MISADVENTURES IN THE SCREEN TRADE

ALISON RIPLEY CUBITT

Lambert Nagle Media

In memory of Mum and Dad, to whom I owe everything.

Copyright © 2022 by Alison Ripley Cubitt All rights reserved.

No part of this book may be reproduced in any form or by any electronic or mechanical means, including information storage and retrieval systems, without written permission from the author, except for the use of brief quotations in a book review.

DISCLAIMER

This is a book written from memory. It reflects my current recollections of experiences over time. Memory isn't one hundred percent infallible, so some dialogue has been recreated. Nearly all the names have been changed and there are characters who are composites of more than one person. Some places and dates have also been changed.

1

My Brilliant Career

Malaysia, 1960s

I'm five years old and at the cinema in Kuala Lumpur, Malaysia with Dad while Mum's in hospital having her appendix out. He's taken me to see *Snow White and the Seven Dwarfs*, but I don't understand a word the wicked Queen is saying. There's been a mix-up, Dad explains. The cinema has received the German version of the film instead of the English one.

I don't care. As the Queen talks into the mirror, '*Spieglein, spieglein an der Wand*,' I can tell by her low, menacing tone that it had better tell her what she wants to hear.

Or else.

That voice gives me nightmares, yet I'm wide awake.

And now I'm going to work for the folks who dreamt up my scariest childhood movie experience. I hope it's not an omen.

* * *

London, 1996

I work in a swanky office in West Kensington with a fancy job title: Producer, Television Specials at Buena Vista Productions, in the TV division of Walt Disney. It's a staff job, with a pension plan, paid holidays and plenty of travel, plus I am invited to film previews and West End shows. For the office Christmas party, Disney books out Madame Tussaud's for the night. I earn more than I ever thought was possible, doing what I love.

'I'll lead on the *Cirque du Monde* project. How about you take *The Making of the Hunchback of Notre Dame?*' my boss Ros says. Ros is a warm-hearted, gregarious sort with Northern roots, maybe ten to fifteen years my senior. She's one of a select few women in senior roles here in London.

Every Disney feature film release in the UK is accompanied by documentary footage as part of the marketing campaign. The USA studios record a version of bland and generic EPK (Electronic Press Kits) stitched together. In Europe, we produce a broadcast-quality 52-minute documentary, in this case commissioned by the BBC and due to be screened on BBC1 on a prime-time early weekend evening slot.

'I'd love to. I'd better read the book,' I say.

'Get the kids' version. I bet that's what Feature Animation read,' Ros says, laughing. I laugh too. 'They're ruffling a few feathers in France.'

I bet they are. *The Hunchback of Notre Dame* is a classic of French literature given the Disney treatment and turned into an animated movie for children.

'I have a director in mind. I've known him for a while, I think you'll get on.' She gives me his card, which I glance at briefly. I've never heard of him. 'He's not done television, but here's his showreel,' Ros says, passing it over. 'He's coming in for a meeting. He'll be here in an hour.'

I return to my desk and watch a couple of the short films. They're beautifully shot and edited, but there's nothing on the showreel that indicates this Director—let's call him Stephen—has worked on any commissions. I fast forward, hoping to find a commercial or a pop video so that I can talk to someone he has worked for and get a second opinion. I'm looking for evidence he can work under pressure. And I don't find it.

How is someone new to TV expected to make the leap from a short film to a commissioned documentary? I don't have the answer to that. But I realise I'm the one who has to make this happen.

When he arrives, Rachel—Ros and my assistant—calls me in for another meeting. She introduces him as Stephen Elwood, the Director working on the project; it turns out that Ros has already hired him. I am blindsided by this turn of events, but remember my manners and greet him with as much enthusiasm as I can muster. So much for me running this project.

'Feature Animation wants to emphasise the collaboration between the French animators in Paris, who are making the opening ten minutes, and their LA colleagues,' Ros says. 'They assume this will help sell the film to the French.' I take notes.

'If we interview the French animators,' I suggest, 'that should give us roughly ten minutes of footage. That's if we can include a clip from the opening sequence?'

'The opening sequence is in the trailer, so it should be okay. While you're in Paris, you could film the gargoyles on Notre Dame Cathedral and the steps.' I scribble down more notes. We have roughly 15 minutes' material for a 52-minute programme. How do we fill the rest of it?

'Can we look at the trailer?' I ask.

'Yes, I'll send a copy through,' Ros says. 'When can we see the film?'

'A week, maybe two, before the edit.'

We're making this blind?

Stephen's eyes widen. 'We don't get to see the actual film until we've finished shooting?'

I wonder if he'd have agreed to do it if he'd known this before.

'You'll have the clips before then. Disney always does it this way. They're terrified of piracy. The films have to be released as close to the official launch as possible. I thought we could have Clopin Trouillefou doing pieces to camera,' Ros adds.

'Who?' Stephen and I say in unison.

'He's the jester, a minor but important character. And Feature Animation is as helpful as the CIA. They won't tell us anything.'

I try to channel Burl Ives singing 'When You Wish Upon A Star.' But all I think of is the Wicked Queen in Snow White.

'Are there plans for a rubber puppet version of Clopin?' Stephen asks.

'Not yet. Just Quasimodo and Esmerelda so far.'

How does a non-existent jester present a programme?

Stephen voices his misgivings when we go back to my office and brainstorm ideas. They mirror mine.

'How about we hire a mime artist from the Jacques Lecoq School in Paris to play the jester? He can bookmark each segment in the programme.'

'We'll be in Paris for the animators, we could film the

mime artist there,' I say. 'Hang on, will you, Stephen? I need to answer this call.'

It'll be either Scarlett or Imogen from Film Marketing. One is blonde and the other brunette, but otherwise they're interchangeable—both patronising and supercilious. Film Marketing is the only London office department that matters in their opinion and Production is merely there to service their needs. And we who run it are the minions.

'We've organised a joint promotion to launch the new Eurostar service to Disneyland, Paris,' Scimogen begins.

'Hang on while I put you on speaker. I've got Stephen, the Director, with me.' I mouth, 'Film Marketing.' He nods.

'We're rarely, rarely excited. You're going to love this.'

I doubt it.

'We're only decorating a Eurostar train with the characters from *The Hunchback of Notre Dame*.' Scimogen pauses for effect, anticipating our awestruck ooh and ahh. We remain silent. 'I mean, how cool is that?'

I shake my head. Stephen does an eye roll. 'That is so exciting,' I say with no enthusiasm.

'I know, right? We've booked stilt walkers, a unicyclist and so many other crazy performers. You know, like...'

'Cirque du Soleil?' Stephen says.

'You've got it. You're so going to love filming that and using it in the documentary.'

It sounds dire. Who the heck do they think is going to come to Waterloo for this?

'We could do that,' I say.

'No, sweetie, you will do that. Guys, we're so going to smash this,' Scimogen says, before hanging up.

'How much of that day's shoot will end up in the finished product, do you think?'

'Thirty seconds. A minute at the most. And that's

pushing it.' Stephen holds his nose and pulls on an imaginary toilet chain.

Sixteen minutes of footage. Thirty-six to go.

* * *

From Malaysia to Ferring-by-Sea, 1960s
An Indian lady folds herself up like a neat parcel, giving a running commentary in Tamil on the black-and-white TV set in the sitting room. I attempt to replicate her antics. Being small, I don't have too far to fall when I crash onto the floor.

We live at Escot, a rubber estate where Dad is the manager in Tanjung Malim in the state of Perak. Malaysia, where I was born, is the place I regard as home.

Shortly after my failed contortionism act, we fly to England. I need an operation to remove my tonsils and adenoids, and Mum wants to be nearer my siblings who are at boarding school there. For a rare treat after my operation, I'm allowed to watch TV in bed. Not only is the telly in English, but there are *two* channels that both make programmes especially for children. I laugh at Johnny Morris in *Animal Magic*, acting as a zookeeper and giving all the animals personalities and silly voices.

While I'm still bed-bound, I hear a pounding on the front door. It's our elderly next-door neighbour; her husband, who is gravely ill, has taken a turn for the worse. The doctor is on his way, but will Mum, who's a nurse, come and see to him? As it's only us at home and I'm still recovering from my operation, she agrees, as long as she can check up on me from time to time.

My bedroom window is at the side of the house, and Mum keeps darting into the neighbour's room opposite, waving to me. I wave back—when I'm not disappearing under the eiderdown, hiding from the Daleks in a terrifying episode of *Dr Who*.

I am too young to know what Mum is really doing next door.

I learn later that when she got there, the poor man was dead, but she still had to wait for the doctor to issue the death certificate. Mum stayed behind to wash the body before the undertakers came. A hearse must have rolled into Ferring Close, but I didn't spot it; I was too busy hoping that the old man in the Tardis (these were the days of the first Dr Who, William Hartnell) would escape his evil tormentors.

Once the summer holidays are over, Mum and I return to Malaysia, where TV hasn't got any better.

* * *

Littlehampton, 1960s
When I turn seven, we travel back to England for me to join my sister at boarding school. Malory Towers it is not; suburban Littlehampton bears no resemblance to Cornish cliffs and windswept beaches.

Another film I insisted Dad took me to when Mum was in hospital was *The Sound of Music*. We went three times. Maria and the other nuns in the film are fun, often bursting into song, but at school, they are mostly miserable. Apart from one. Like Maria, Sister Carmel is both young and joyful. A Carmelite nun before she came to teach us at the Holy Family Convent, she explains that her former order is a silent one.

No wonder she didn't like it there. She never stops talking.

We spend weekend afternoons in winter huddled around the black-and-white television set. This is the only time we're allowed to watch TV. It's best when Sister Carmel is in charge. She lets us watch *Top of the Pops*.

* * *

Mariri, South Island, New Zealand
When we emigrate to New Zealand in 1968, after Dad is made redundant from his job in Malaysia, it feels like we've gone back in time. There's only one TV channel and it screens endless repeats of British programmes we've already seen. At least some of the American sitcoms are new to us: *Mr Ed*, the talking horse, and Arnold, the pig from *Petticoat Junction*, who visit the folks in *Green Acres*; and *The Beverly Hillbillies*. The apple and pear orchard where we live is six miles from town, and until I can gain my driving licence at age fifteen, I'm stuck at home in the evenings. Once I finish riding and then homework, TV is the default option.

My classmates are told 'Telly leads to delinquency' and that if you sit there all night in front of the box, you'll never amount to anything. But for me, watching TV is family time with Dad, especially when it's just us in the house as Mum works night shifts at the maternity hospital in Motueka. We watch comedies together like *The Morecambe and Wise Show*, *The Two Ronnies,* and anything that Tommy Cooper appears in. I like factual programmes like *World in Action* and *Panorama*. As a teenager in the 1970s, I learn more about World War II from the 26-part documentary series *The World at War* than I ever would in the classroom.

Mum and Dad want to send me to a different secondary school to the one my siblings attend, but their alternative, Waimea College, is a three-hour round trip by bus in term time. I choose the nearest, Motueka High School. It has a restricted curriculum of English, French, Geography, Maths,

Sciences and Sports; I am sad there's no drama, but I'm not bothered about missing out on music. My sister is the musical one.

The most important lesson I learn is that if you want to be somebody, you need to leave our small town, where not much happens, and head for the big city. And the school facilitates this by sending me off on a weeklong career course, 250 km away across Cook Strait in Wellington, North Island. I have to pick ten employers from the list the school hands me, but I only want to visit the exciting ones—in advertising, broadcasting and newspapers. To make up the numbers, I sling in some random government departments and companies on the list.

As I wait outside Radio New Zealand, my heart skips a beat. The little group of students I am with are ushered into a meeting room. A smartly dressed woman wearing a skirt suit gives the presentation, and from what she says, it sounds like the station pays you to entertain and inform people. But then comes the stinger: for radio and especially television, you need a degree. And that's only the start.

I don't know anybody who works in advertising, broadcasting, newspapers or radio, so there's no one to ask for guidance or advice. Mum and Dad have a network of friends and relatives, but none of them have jobs that involve writing or performance. Now I've found out that there is such a thing as a career in the media, I know what I want to do with my life.

I guess it's time to start paying more attention in class.

* * *

Wellington, North Island At nine in the morning after the last of my university finals, I'm sitting in a lecture theatre in downtown Wellington with a raging hangover. In front of me is an electronic keyboard with a loose cover. I lift the cover, slip my hands underneath as instructed and place my fingers on the keys, ready to start.

When I glance down, I can't see my fingers. How am I going to know which key is which?

Projected onto the screen at the front of the lecture room is a giant typewriter. All I have to do is follow the instructions of the cheerful American voice-over man, and at the end of the course, I'll be able to touch-type 60 words per minute. Or that's the theory. My head is throbbing and I'm scared I'll throw up at any moment. When Voice-over Man reels off which letters on the now obscured keyboard to press, I can't keep up.

By the following Friday, I've managed 40 wpm and scrape through with a pass. A week's training will hardly put me in the same league as Mum, who at sixteen studied shorthand and typing at secretarial college for six months and, despite ditching the office job for a nursing career thirty years ago, can still type faster than me. She's kept up her shorthand too, which comes in handy for shopping lists and private notes that only she can read.

In stark contrast to Mum, I wrote all my university essays using the two-finger hunt-and-peck method on a manual typewriter. I have no intention of becoming a secretary, but an ability to type might make me more employable; the only marketable skill I previously possessed is that I can drive. My ability to make a white sauce without a recipe, carry three plates at once and ride a horse (though not all at the same time) doesn't offer much in the way of career options.

That I have a degree at all is nothing short of miraculous. I got off to a rocky start, flailing around in my first semester on the wrong course, then switching not only universities, but cities. And as I was about to start my exams in my second year, my father, who suffered from clinical depression, took his own life. I fell apart and took a semester off, retreating to home to grieve.

There is nothing to keep me in Wellington, but because I have a non-vocational degree, there are no opportunities back at home, either. When a friend plans her move to Sydney, somewhere I love, I ask to tag along. And in an act of extraordinary selflessness, my widowed mother urges me to go. I am not to worry about her, she tells me.

This will be a hard habit to break. Since I was a teenager, I've felt like my mother's keeper. But since my grandmother has moved in with Mum, I give myself permission to let this responsibility go. For now.

For most of my three years at Victoria University of Wellington (Vic), I lived in a flat near the main campus on the hill in Kelburn. From my bedroom, I watched planes in the distance land and take off. I vowed that one day, I'd be on one. As we hurtle down the runway, I realise this is it; there's no going back. I'm breaking away—fleeing as far as I can from my fractured family.

But that's not the only reason I'm leaving: I'm running towards something. If only I could figure out what that is.

* * *

Sydney 1981
Here I am at the Sydney Hilton in George Street, wearing my black uniform, menu in one hand, wine list in the other, fronting up to a table of business executives, all men.

'Yes,' I told the interviewer who gave me the job, not entirely truthfully, 'the last restaurant on my CV was Silver Service.' This is the marker of a pretentious restaurant where deferential waiting staff serve each diner with vegetables from silver dishes. It requires an elaborate sleight of hand with cutlery, more skill than I possess. But I have practised at home using two spoons to serve peas.

I stand, pen in hand, poised to take the men's drinks order. They ask for two bottles of Moët & Chandon Brut Impérial champagne. As I run off down the swelteringly hot corridor, head down, worrying that I'll have to open both bottles in front of the customers, a large brown rat comes scampering boldly towards me. I wish I were that confident. I move towards the wine storage. The rat goes in the other direction, attracted by the pungent acidic smell of cockroach.

If only the customers knew what lurks in these corridors.

I find the right champagne and scuttle back along the corridor, the two bottles of precious bubbly firmly in my grasp. My hands shake, but I disguise my trembling by draping the linen napkin over my left arm. I turn the label of the first bottle to the host and he nods.

Placing the second bottle in an ice-bucket, I start to open the first. From the pocket in my uniform, I pull out the Waiter's Friend corkscrew, flick it open, prise the wire from around the cork and peel off the silver foil, all without cutting myself. So far, so good.

I twist the cork. It's stuck fast.

I twist the bottle. The cork won't budge.

I try again. My cheeks feel hot, but it's nothing to do with the temperature. The men at the table shift in their seats. One looks poised to grab the bottle from me.

I'll show him.

I turn away, wedge the champagne bottle between my knees, and twist the cork. My left hand stops it from flying out. I grab the nearest glass and pour the champagne before it erupts like a lava flow all over the table, then move methodically around the guests.

Not a drop spilt. I hope they're good tippers.

As I turn to head for the kitchen to fetch the starters, I see out of the corner of my eye the death stare of the restaurant manager. I carry on with a sinking feeling in my stomach. My career prospects with this particular establishment don't look good at this moment.

At the end of the shift, he fires me.

Deciding that hospitality is too much like hard work for little reward, I approach an office temping agency. I am promptly sent to the Finance Department at Best & Less in Leichhardt, only I mishear the company's name and keep calling it Best & Lest.

Best & Less don't have tills. The company uses an elaborate system of pressurised air tubes built into the ceiling that whizzes money and receipts through the building. The checkout operator puts the customer's money and a paper order into a capsule and sends it up the tube to Accounts. We in Accounts open the tube, work out the change needed and return the capsule to the shop floor.

Unsurprisingly, I am not trusted with tube duty. I don't trust myself, either; why an arts graduate who only managed 52% in Maths at School Certificate on her second attempt is a good fit for Customer Accounts at a budget department store, I can't fathom. I would probably mix up which counter is which or give the wrong change. Instead, I have to reconcile the takings for the day, adding up all the receipts to make sure they tally. But they never do.

The only light relief in my tedious job comes at lunchtime. I spend my hour's break ploughing up and down the main drag, looking for inexpensive sandwich bars until I discover Norton Street, off Parramatta Road. Leichhardt in the 1980s caters to the Italian community who immigrated to Australia after World War II, and Norton Street is awash with family-run Italian restaurants serving the lunchtime crowds; for almost the same price as a take-away sandwich, I can sit down at a table with a bowl of spaghetti.

I've only experienced the beautiful Italian language spoken via the magic of the movies at the Wellington Film Festival and in film studies at university. What a difference to hear the language in real life; the accents are completely unlike those on screen for a start and I can barely understand a word of what the other patrons are saying. The reason for this, it turns out, is that they're not speaking Italian, but dialects from the various regions: Calabria, Campania and Sicily.

When Italian families first migrated to Australia, one or two from a village would arrive and, if all went well, they would encourage their compatriots to join them. The new immigrants then had a community ready to welcome them; they were given support to find jobs and somewhere to live, as well as help with learning English. I'm fascinated to learn about this vibrant community as I enjoy my daily pasta.

However, much as I love spending time with the Italians, an hour's escape every day from the tedium of trying to tally till receipts is not enough to save me. I keep making errors, even though I use a calculator for every transaction. At the end of my first week, I am told that my services are no longer required.

Just as well. Along with that generous lunchtime bowlful of spaghetti, I've discovered the Italian ice-cream shops and I have been buying a gelato after work, trying a different flavour every day. If I were to stay in Leichhardt any longer, I'd be the size of a small house. Best & Lest have done me a favour.

2

Mad Men

Sydney 1981
When I apply for a position as a receptionist in a medium-sized advertising agency in North Sydney, I tell Melanie, the boss's secretary who interviews me, that although I have a degree, I'm happy to start at the bottom. This will give me an insight into the business, and then I can work my way up from there.

'Which area would you prefer to be in?' she asks.

'The one that makes ads, the creative side.'

What's it called again?

'I'd like to be a copywriter.'

'For now, we need a receptionist. If you prove yourself there, we'll see.'

How long will "we'll see" take?

I'm too young to understand that what the company needs and what I want aren't necessarily compatible.

So my career in advertising begins, in a somewhat less glamourous way than I'd hoped. I sit at reception, operate the switchboard, take phone messages, as well as meet and greet clients. Because it's always busy, I'm not allowed to leave reception, even to go to the loo, without asking a colleague to cover for me.

My desk faces out into the foyer. Behind me is the boardroom, which has an oval table in the middle surrounded by a dozen chairs. On one side is a bar and a fridge. Every day, I have to replenish it with wine and beer, spirits, mixers, ice, nuts and miscellaneous snacks. If there are breakfast or lunch meetings, I order in and lay out the plates and the cutlery. There is a drip filter coffee machine, which is only for senior staff and visitors—and me. My one perk is I'm allowed to help myself. Richard, the boss, drinks at least eight cups a day. I'm constantly topping it up.

As well as makeshift caterer, my job description includes gopher—when I'm not collecting dry-cleaning, I'm watering plants or buying birthday cards. Occasionally, I'm given some agency work.

The guy who works for the Media Department looks like he just walked off the set of a Ralph Lauren photoshoot, his white linen shirts and bright primary coloured trousers pristine as he leans over my desk and instructs me in the ways of typing up the media bookings. I have a piece of A3 paper for print ads, and another for radio and television. It takes ages to position each sheet so that it's perfectly aligned and straight in the electric typewriter. I put an X in a grid next to the name of the relevant magazine or newspaper, and then do the same for radio and TV airtime ads, but the potential for costly mistakes in the latter is beyond terrifying. If I put the X in the incorrect square in the grid, I could end up booking the ad on the wrong day or, worse still, the wrong channel. With a lot of concentration and probably a little luck, I catch all my errors in time.

When I make a mistake, I have to pull out the paper and dab it with a little brush from a pot of correction fluid. Then it's literally a matter of waiting for paint to dry before re-inserting the sheet into the typewriter to repeat the rigmarole of lining it up again. If the paint hasn't dried properly, I end up with an illegible grey splodge and I have to retype the whole thing again.

The firm is owned and run by business partners, Richard and Yasmin, who I guess to be in their fifties. Richard is British and has a history with top London agencies, while Yasmin has worked her way up the ranks in Australia. They are married, but not to each other, even though they always come to work together.

Richard and Yasmin conduct their meetings in the late afternoons and are not to be disturbed under any circumstances. I write in large letters in my desk diary that the boardroom is booked for this time, and if any of the other staff forget to check and are stupid enough to try to go in there, I leap up from my chair and stand against the door like a bouncer.

At the appointed time, Yasmin's geometric bracelets clang like wayward tectonic plates about to cause an earthquake as she wafts past reception under a sickly sweet cloud of bergamot, mandarin, myrrh and jasmine in her figure-hugging skirt suit, her blouse unbuttoned to reveal her ample cleavage, her black bob blow-dried to perfection. It must take her forever to get ready for work every morning. And when she leaves the boardroom after a "meeting" with Richard, she's generally still adjusting her clothing as she walks back to her office.

If it gets busy at reception, the chat drowns out the curious moans and groans coming from the boardroom, but when Yasmin's bracelets ring out like the bell on a doomed ship, I just about hold it together as I answer calls in my best telephone voice. If it's only me at the desk, I can usually keep up an air of serious professionalism, but if another colleague is passing and we glance at each other, that's it. The agency's worst kept secret is out of the bag, again.

In advertising, image is everything. As the receptionist is the first point of contact at the agency, how I sound and look is paramount. So when, after six months, Melanie pulls me aside and tells me that Richard wants to talk to me, my head is full of possible scenarios.

Either he's about to fire or promote me.

When he proposes to give me a clothing allowance so that I will project a smarter image, I'm floored. That's probably the one scenario that didn't go through my mind. He tells me he's happy with my telephone voice and says I got hired because I don't sound Australian.

I assume he's trying to pay me a compliment.

Naturally, Richard goes on to intimate, the allowance will come with strings attached. Melanie is to accompany me on my shopping trip, as this is company money and it has to be spent wisely. I like Melanie—I feel that we're on the same side, but we're opposites when it comes to clothes. She combines tasteful cream linen skirts and matching pumps with pastel-coloured blouses, a wide belt and delicate jewellery pulling the look together, while I only own one "office" dress: a striped number that fits me well. All my other outfits are in various shades of black, which I team with scarves and leggings. This ensemble may have worked at university, but the agency favours heels, skirts, and dresses.

I struggle to come up with a suitable answer for Richard. It seems he believes his offer is a kind one, or at least nothing out of the ordinary, but for me, it's humiliating. What if I accept his offer, and then get a new job? I'll be indebted to the company and have to pay back money I spent on clothes I never wanted. If Richard gives me an allowance to buy work outfits, he'll demand the maximum return for his investment and I'll be stuck in reception, going nowhere. And if I can't even be trusted to choose my own clothes, when are he and Yasmin going to allow me to write ad copy for their clients?

Thinking about what I see when I look around at work, I realise that the women do the boring jobs in the agency while the men get to do the creative stuff. Maybe I've been blind-sided by Yasmin and the fact that she's in a position of power. Perhaps the best thing I can do is get out while I still can. It seems that advertising in 1980s Australia is very much a boys' club; do I have the fight in me to take them on?

I ask Richard for time to think about it.

3

Newsfront

Spurred on to find a better-paid graduate job, I answer an ad for a radio and television news monitor at the Haymarket end of George Street, between Chinatown and Central Station. After the sterility of corporate North Sydney, I'm relieved to be back in the beating heart of the city.

After the flak I received about my appearance from the image-obsessed advertising industry, I choose a smart-casual suit for the interview. But I look overdressed as the managers are in jeans, shirts and jumpers. The only people who smarten up are the Marketing team who have face-to-face contact with clients.

This is not a problem for me; it doesn't take any time for me to adjust to dressing down. And as well as being able to wear whatever I like, I don't have to work standard nine-to-five office hours, which suits me down to the ground.

As the business is expanding, Jackie, one of the managers, has been on a recruitment drive and hired three new members of staff: Paul, in Sydney on a gap year from the UK; Sophia, a journalism graduate using this as a stepping stone to a PR career; and me. I'm just grateful to be working in a media job that will take me places. I don't yet know where those places are, but I'm learning fast.

The team I join operates like a newsroom across seven days a week in case a story breaks. But although the Print Monitors start work at some ungodly hour when the morning editions of the newspapers roll off the presses, the earliest start for us Broadcast Monitors is 7am. We rely on state-of-the-art recording equipment, which is primed to tape overnight radio programmes. Our shifts alternate between morning and afternoon, and we each have to work every third Sunday.

On the early shift, we finish by 2pm, and in summer, we're able to go to the beach. We don't have a lunch hour, preferring to work straight through even though our bosses would rather we took a break. Their argument is that we might miss something if we get too tired, so we set out to prove them wrong—showing that we get better rest from a longer gap between shifts.

The late shift starts at 1pm, which allows for an hour's handover and a briefing. We talk about the breaking stories involving any of our clients, and where the coverage is likely to be. Then we record all programmes we are to monitor on video and radio cassette to be able to quote accurately when there are specific mentions and interviews. The tapes also serve as a legal record in case any of the interviewees or shock jocks try to deny what they've said.

The first task on the early shift is to check that the night crew remembered to insert all the audio and video cassette tapes to record breakfast news and current affairs programmes. While we wait for those to finish, we listen to the cassettes and video tapes from the night before. The audio cassettes record 60 minutes per side, and at the end of the hour, I have to remember to turn them over.

With headphones on, I can't hear the hissing from the audio tapes when they jam up, which means winding the tape back in with the help of a pencil to try to salvage the recording. But if the tape spools out everywhere, it's too late to fix it. Video tapes aren't so temperamental and luckily, there are back-ups.

Our job after listening to the tapes is to log and summarise every item in the broadcast, taking particular note of any mention of our clients. As the client lists keep changing, the names are written on a whiteboard as a reminder. At 9am, Julie, whose job is Client Liaison, arrives, and by then we need to have rattled through enough programmes to keep her busy. She then alerts the relevant PR departments to any negative news stories as early in the day as possible to give them a chance to respond in time for the evening news bulletins, but in a 24-hour news cycle, stories don't always break at convenient times. If there's an unfolding story, Julie tells us and we watch or listen live, while she waits anxiously in the background, ready to call the client the moment we've finished summarising the salient points.

The worst crime we can commit is missing a client interview; a lesser one is to miss a mention. It happens to all of us at some stage, but repeat offenders (luckily not me) are hauled into Jackie's office and given a verbal warning.

When Julie takes time off, we take turns to cover for her. A few days before her holiday when it's my turn to cover, I listen in to a client conversation, making a mental note to mirror the way she sells them the negative coverage. When I'm in the hot seat, though, I get off lightly as all I have to do is read out a summary before sending the written reports by courier. But even Julie struggles with one particular client, who she has to ring every day, story or no story.

Abe Saffron is the Mr Big of organised crime in Sydney and controls all the gambling and prostitution in the vice dens in King's Cross. When someone goes missing and winds up dead, the finger of blame inevitably turns to him. Abe does his own PR, so poor Julie has to report to the man himself.

When Julie rings Abe, we pretend to be busy, but we're all listening in, sending her sympathy vibes as she reads out the latest allegations of who he is supposed to have killed. He always wants direct quotes and insists on knowing the names of interviewees and the reporter. It's not difficult to guess why.

I wouldn't want to be that journalist.

The job I dislike the most is monitoring talkback (or racist radio) as most of us in the office are immigrants or the children of them. Controversial talkback host Ron Casey eggs on his listeners to call in and make derogatory and disrespectful remarks about indigenous Australians and immigrants. Unfortunately, his message goes down well with his listeners. On the afternoon shift on a quiet news day, it doesn't get busy until after Julie leaves to do the school run. At 5pm, the radio current affairs programmes kick in. A few minutes before the main TV news bulletins start at six, I insert videos into the machines, ready to press the record button for the evening broadcasts. At 6.30pm, I jump up to tape the major news bulletins on other channels. But if I want to leave the office on time, I have to race through two commercial channels in fifteen minutes each, as ABC News, the most comprehensive bulletin of them all, must be watched live. It's a relentless feat of concentration as there are no ad breaks in that bulletin, but I have a breather during the sport and weather reports.

I place two A4 notepads on the desk, ready for watching

the commercial channels live at the same time. In theory, it can be done; there are three ad breaks in the commercial channels' bulletins where I catch up. For big international stories, such as the Falklands War footage, all I need to do is to record the length of the clip and the subject. For local content, I write the name of the interviewee and add in their quote verbatim.

This is where it gets tricky watching two channels at the same time. With packaged clips, each channel puts its own spin on what the interviewee says; if I rush my report and get the direct quotes wrong or, heaven forbid, misspell their name, it's sod's law that the client will be at home watching.

By 7.30pm, I feel like I've been through the ringer, but I still have another recorded bulletin to get through. After that, I read through my hand-written notes to make sure they're legible and place the labelled tapes on Julie's desk. Then I do a quick tidy up of any papers lying around on the desks before I insert audio tapes into the machines ready for the morning. After work, as I don't have to be back until the following lunchtime, I can go to movies, clubs, or dinners, knowing that I can have a lie-in the next day.

The Sunday shift starts at midday. When it's my turn, I'm alone in the building, which can be creepy. For the first couple of hours, I have nothing to do, apart from eating a leisurely lunch and reading the newspaper while trying not to imagine burglars breaking in, ready to attack a lone news monitor. I hear every creak, and if a door slams, I leap up, terrified. It takes me ages to pluck up the courage to investigate, but it usually turns out that someone forgot to close a window properly and the door got caught in the breeze.

But who am I expecting to break in? In this part of town near Central Station, drug addicts, I guess, looking for cash. By 5pm on a Sunday, I'm too busy to worry about imaginary intruders, and my headphones block out any external noise anyway. There could be a party full of drug addicts going on downstairs and I wouldn't hear anything.

Nursing a terrible hangover one Sunday morning after being out clubbing until 2am, I decide to take a little snooze under my desk. I'm so out of it, even the carpet looks comfortable. However, I have barely dozed off before the sound of a key in the door wakes me from my slumber. My vantage point under the desk allows me to spot a man from the knees down, walking towards me. I recognise his shoes. They belong to the big boss, the owner of the company.

I haul myself up, patting down the cheap felt carpet tiles, pretending to look for an imaginary contact lens. He offers to help. The next thing I know, he's on the floor, searching too. When we find nothing apart from a few dead flies and cockroach droppings, I thank him profusely and sit at my desk, squinting and praying he'll pick up whatever it was he came in for and leave.

Much as I enjoy my job and the socialising, especially hanging out with Paul and Sophia, I'm tired of King's Cross and all its sleaze. Potts Point where I'm living is barely a hundred metres from Abe Saffron's empire in the Cross, and at weekends, the red-light district is grim. Suburbanites regard the Cross as a tourist attraction and come to gawp at the hookers. At 3am, patrons still roar up and down the streets in their noisy modified cars. Drunken mobs spill out of the Bourbon and Beefsteak pub and Les Girls nightclub, looking for some late-night action. But most of the hardcore business takes place later at night, long after the tourists have gone home, when it's safer to walk along the main drag than risk taking a poorly lit side-street.

I live for a while with Catriona, whose angelic features perfectly suit her short, spiky hair. To deter the doormen waiting outside the red-light clubs from propositioning us, we pretend that we're a couple. We figure that even if this strategy doesn't work, at least they'll look out for us when we eventually stagger home.

The apartment we live in on Macleay Street is on the eighth floor of an art deco building, and my bedroom faces the street. During the week, even though the windows are single-glazed, most nights I sleep right through. But one night, I'm woken with a start when a blood-curdling scream rings out.

Leaning out the window and seeing a man dragging a woman by her long, dark hair, I then run to get my flatmate. She heard it too.

'Come on, let's go,' she says, wrapping a dressing gown round her and grabbing her slippers. Catriona may be small, but she's feisty. Motivated by adrenaline and fear, I take my cue from her and do the same.

There's no time to think. As we dash out of the building towards the attacker, he tries to pull the woman into a car. We pummel him until he releases her.

He turns, walking away empty-handed, yelling obscenities. I am shaking as he gets into the passenger seat of the car, thinking how easily our intervention could have gone wrong.

What if he had been armed?

4

Don't Look Now

Florence, 1982

In September, I arrive at Rome's Fiumicino railway station, having flown for over 24 hours from Sydney. After listening to my heavily accented Italian, the ticket seller sends me off to the train to Faenza. I realise my mistake and have to run for the train to Firenze, only to catch the stopping one instead of the express.

I'm hoping that an educational holiday in Italy, soaking up as much of the language, art, and culture as I'm able to cram in, will give me the breathing space to contemplate my future. The course I have picked is both the cheapest and the most intensive, but the delivery of it is too dry for me as it focuses on the written language rather than conversation. In the afternoon, we're expected to revise the grammar we've learned and do all the homework we've been set. We do at least have to speak only in Italian from the moment we walk into the class at 9am until we leave at midday. Nonetheless, I soon lose my enthusiasm and struggle to keep up.

I have taken lodgings in a *pensione* in the centre of Florence, near to the Duomo. To cut costs, I share a room;

my room-mate is a fresh-faced Swiss girl of eighteen, who I nickname Heidi. She switches off her light at 9pm and is up with the lark at 6am. She too is here to learn Italian, which is just as well as this is the only language we have in common.

There are no cooking facilities in our room and it offers nowhere to eat our take-away meals apart from on our beds. Heidi exists on apples; I live on take-away pizza. Weekdays are busy with language school and homework, but it's evenings and weekends in the cramped accommodation I find tough. Usually, I try to stay out as late as possible. Other times, I park myself in reception, writing letters while the television, which is always on, drones away in the background.

At weekends, I wander around the art galleries or the market, or catch a train to explore other parts of Tuscany and Umbria. I live for the one weekend every month when Heidi goes home to Switzerland. For two blissful days, I'll eat pizza and drink wine, loving that once again I have the luxury of a room of my own, even if it is short-lived.

I don't recall where I meet Dawn, a Grace Jones lookalike from Brixton, who has a job as a nanny. She learned her Italian in Milan before relocating to Florence, and will switch from her best Sarf-London 'You know what I mean?' to fluent Italian in an instant. To suggest that we make an odd-looking pair is an understatement, especially when I get my hair cut and coloured in town. Instead of highlighting it, the hairdresser bleaches it all white blonde. Florence at the time is provincial and ultra conservative, so I didn't exactly blend in when my hair was highlighted; now I've turned into a Debbie Harry clone, it's far worse. When I stand next to Dawn, who is close to six foot and favours a flat-top hairstyle teamed with punky outfits, we literally bring traffic to a standstill. Men leer out of their car windows and offer us lifts; even the ones going in the opposite direction will do a U-turn and promise to drive us anywhere we want. Usually, we refuse, having learned our lesson the hard way.

While still relatively naïve, we accepted a lift from a man tempting us with an outing to the countryside. Dawn immediately took charge of the conversation and things were going well—until, inevitably, he propositioned her. In response, she pretended she was a devout Catholic with a pressing need to visit the nearest church to pray to the Madonna. For some reason—I can't think why—the driver didn't buy her story, so Dawn resorted to Plan B and drew upon her extensive repertoire of Milanese swear words. When these developed into insults about the man's mother and manhood (I'm not sure which he regarded as the more offensive), he got so angry, he slammed on his brakes and dumped us in the middle of nowhere. We had no choice but to walk to the nearest lay-by and stick out our thumbs, praying that the next person who stopped wouldn't be another psycho.

Unwanted attention from male drivers isn't the only way in which my three months' extended holiday doesn't quite go according to plan. In October 1982, Italian bank employees vote for industrial action. I left my savings in my Australian bank account to transfer as and when I needed them, but once the bank strikes start, to my horror, the staff refuse to let me withdraw any cash. It feels unfair as I've spent the previous two years saving for what is supposed to be a break. Mum offers to help, but the only way to do this is via a bank transfer, which the banks refuse to process. Even if she could help me out financially, I would feel guilty accepting money from her; since she became a widow, she and my grandmother have lived together on a limited income.

Now I'm down and out in Florence, I investigate all the free outings. Many of these trips involve visits to churches, including Santa Croce and San Lorenzo. I enrolled in a Renaissance Art and Architecture paper at university in Wellington, but had to abandon it when I dropped out after Dad died. My interest in the subject is still strong, though, and I relish the one Sunday in the month when the Uffizi gallery is free. At uni, we studied all the artworks as slides, so this is the first time I have ever seen an Italian Renaissance painting in all its glory. I stand, transfixed, in front of Botticelli's *The Birth of Venus*; I'd naively imagined it as a painting you could put above a mantlepiece, but it occupies an entire wall.

Too ashamed to tell anyone else, I keep the news that I have no money to myself. Every day, I visit the bank and ask the staff if the funds have come through; every day, a teller shrugs and says, 'Impossible.' I try not to cry in front of the bank staff, but sometimes it's difficult. Here I am, far from home, trying to explain in another language that my savings are my only income. Breakfast is coffee and biscuits from the supermarket and the cheapest food I find for dinner is pizza sold by the slice. My only treat is a bottle of the local red wine which I eke out for as long as possible, and on weekends, I have saved enough from my diminishing funds to splurge on a gelato.

When I pluck up the courage to confess what's going on, the elderly sisters who own the *pensione* take pity on me and allow me to run up an account until the strike is over. A classmate, an undergraduate from Stanford in California, extends a helping hand which I'll never forget. She withdraws cash from her American Express credit card account and lends it to me, which tides me over for a month until the rolling strikes are finally over. It's a lesson learned: this experience teaches me that I can't just rely on banks.

When the strike is over, the first thing I do after paying my debts is return to the indoor Mercato Centrale on Via dell'Ariento to buy a black leather jacket that I scoped out weeks ago. I don't know how it still fits me, as I have since gained 5kg through stress and all the unhealthy food I've consumed. That evening, I take myself out to a restaurant and order some protein with a side order of salad. It takes years before I eat pizza again.

Fortunately for me, the *pensione* attracts a fair number of backpackers so there is always someone new in town who wants company in the evenings. There are strict rules in place—it's women-only and men are only permitted as far as reception. Because the sisters who run it lock the front door at 11pm, I'm often to be spotted legging it down the pavement, running late. Now my finances are sorted, Friday and Saturday nights are for partying.

* * *

Venice, 1982
When two Australian sisters, Rosemary and Jill, invite me on a weekend break to Venice, I jump at the chance. We hit it off as soon as they arrived at the *pensione*, and I'm not going to turn down the chance to see such an iconic place in good company.

We have to pay for a night's accommodation, but because it's November and the off-season, we get a good deal. We set off on the early train on Saturday morning, arrive at lunchtime and dump our stuff in our triple room. If I'd been there on my own, I'd have gone looking for artworks by Titian and Tintoretto and all the other Venetian Renaissance painters. But as I have company and the sun's reflection is sparkling on the Venetian lagoon, despite it being late autumn, we choose people-watching at a cafe over viewing art treasures in stuffy churches.

It must be fairly obvious to the locals that we're tourists, as it's not long before three uniformed Carabinieri officers, taking a lunch break at a nearby table, approach. They are very polite and ask in English if we would like a drink. We hesitate and glance at each other, but not wishing to be rude, we agree.

Once they've bought our drinks, they come over to the table. They ask what we all do and Rosemary blurts out that we're professional musicians and are members of a trio. It isn't totally untrue; Rosemary and Jill are students at a music school in Rome. It's just me lying to the Italian police.

I keep quiet, hoping to discover what instrument I play. The sisters decide that I'm a violinist, which comes as news to me as the only instrument I play (badly) is the piano. But it seems the cops are taken in and offer to give us a tour of the Venetian lagoon on their police launch after work. That sounds tempting, but we're not sure how we're going to get rid of them afterwards. And then one offers to drive me around the Veneto region in his Alpha Giulietta, of which he is very proud.

That's a step too far. 'Thank you,' I say, thinking quickly, 'but I can't abandon my sisters.'

'*Sorelle?*'

'*Si, sorelle. Mia sorelle,*' I say loudly. Rosemary and Jill catch on and nod vigorously.

That is yet another lie that I've told a police officer. He looks at me, then at my "sisters." I don't resemble them in the slightest; I hope he's not trained in facial recognition and that as far as he's concerned, all blonde Antipodeans look alike.

The officers reluctantly finish their lunch and head off to their patrol boat. We three agree that for the remainder of the weekend, we'll keep a low profile away from the Grand, the small and all the other canals in case we have the bad luck to encounter them again. But being in Venice at the weekend, we soon throw caution aside and head to a bar and seafood restaurant. Everywhere is heaving, so the maître d' asks if we'd mind sharing a table and points towards three men who quite simply look like Nordic gods.

We don't mind at all.

Nor do they, it appears. It turns out they are not actually Nordic, but Italians from Trentino-Alto Adige on the border with Austria, which accounts for the fair hair. They are law students, in Venice for the weekend just like we are. We're so busy enjoying their company as the evening wears on that we don't notice the group of cops we encountered earlier, now out of uniform. They've certainly noticed us, though, and are waving in our direction from across the room.

Awkward.

I nudge Jill. 'What do we do?'

'Wave back,' she urges.

'It's easy for you; that one with the Alpha is way too persistent. I'm not going on that tour of the countryside with him.' I turn to our new buddies. 'Guys, we're in a bit of an awkward situation. There are some Carabinieri over there, and the one with the moustache keeps on asking me out. I don't want to offend them, especially as they're cops, but...'

Luciano, whose English is the best of the three not-Nordic gods, turns around. 'Yeah, they look like off-duty cops. Too neat.' He grins. 'I get it – you'd rather not spend a night in a jail cell with three lecherous Carabinieri.'

'How did you guess? Uh-oh, they're coming over.'

Luciano puts his arm around me and the other two guys sit close to the sisters.

'We lied to them and said we are a musical troupe. I play the violin,' I say just as the beaming cops arrive. Struggling to keep a straight face, Luciano leaps up and greets them like long-lost friends, offering them a seat at our table. His companions have caught on and are playing their part to great effect, snuggling up to the sisters.

This proves too much for the police officers. Their smiles vanishing, they say a curt goodbye and retreat, while we order another bottle of Prosecco and toast our narrow escape. Before long, we have lost all track of time.

'How about we pay up and take a wander?' I say, hoping the fresh air will clear my head; the fizz has made me giddy. But Venice at night in November is sinister; the landmarks we'd noticed in the daylight seem to have disappeared in the gloom. There is a biting chill and a cold, damp fog swirls around us.

'This way,' Jill calls out. 'I'm sure of it. We passed that little bridge there.'

'You're sure? One bridge looks like any other to me.'

Especially when I've drunk this much fizz.

We round the corner. The footpath slopes down and abruptly stops, submerged in the lapping waters of yet another impassable canal. After a lot more stumbling down darkened streets, only to retrace our steps as our path is cut off, we finally find our way out of the maze and onto the narrow street where the lights of our *pensione* still shine.

Rosemary pipes up, 'We need to make a run for it, or else we'll be locked out.' I look at my watch: 11.55pm, and the doors close at midnight. Rosemary rushes off with Jill trailing behind her.

'I can't run in these,' I say, looking down at my heeled boots and the uneven paving. Much to our escorts' amusement, I then pull off my boots and dash after the sisters, like some latter-day Cinderella. In the distance, I see Rosemary and the owner of our lodgings gesticulating down the street in our direction. We must look quite a sight, me and the not-Nordic gods, as the owner turns on her heels, followed by the unmistakeable sound of the heavy metal front door clanging shut.

Not good.

Rosemary and Jill walk sorrowfully back. 'She wasn't having a bar of it. And she's still going to charge for the room,' Rosemary says.

'Come with us,' Luciano says. 'There's bound to be somewhere open.' But what I notice is how deserted the place looks. After this amount of wine, my language skills are no longer up to pleading for a room at the inn. And the guys are no help: they haven't even got around to checking into a hotel, having headed straight for the bar on arrival in Venice.

We retrace our footsteps, but hotel after hotel is closed for the night; even the chain ones are in darkness. We ring the bell at a few, and Luciano produces wads of notes out of his pocket and pleads with a night manager.

'Why can't we sleep in the foyer on the sofas and armchairs?' he asks.

Each manager shakes their head and repeats the same words: 'Non è possible.'

A shiver goes down my spine. We are facing the genuine prospect of spending the night in a deck chair in St Mark's Square. The damp fog is seeping into my bones, it's 1.30am and we are all feeling exhausted. In the darkness, we lose our bearings again. The path runs out and the only sound is the water lapping against a line of tied-up gondolas.

'How about we sleep in one of those?' Luciano suggests. 'That big one there should fit all of us. Look, the cover's loose. If we just pull that off, we can sneak in. By the time the gondolier comes to work in the morning, we'll have gone.'

We turn to each other. Why not? After all, we've run out of options.

Luciano's two friends get on board. One sits at the bow and the other at the stern. The sisters and I clamber aboard with the help of Luciano. The gondola rocks a little, but with the weight spread evenly, we are at least able to sit down.

On the water, it's colder still. Even the cover doesn't provide much protection from the elements. Luciano, who is wearing a thick Afghan coat, takes it off and gently places it over our shoulders. Trying to share out the warmth, we huddle together, turning his coat into a makeshift rug.

I turn towards Rosemary. 'This'll be a story to tell in 20 years' time. My night in a Venetian gondola.'

'Ha, ha, ha.' And then she looks at me. 'All we need now is for someone to dob us in, call the cops and tell them that we've broken into a gondola.'

'I can see it now, those Carabinieri from earlier, roaring down the Grand Canal on their patrol boat to arrest the three wayward Antipodeans who spurned them.'

One day, I am sure, we'll be able to look back and laugh.

It's 6am on Sunday. As the others stir, bleary-eyed, I leap up, overcome with motion sickness, desperate to get out of that boat.

'We'd better make a move before someone spots us,' Luciano says. It's dark still and the only sound comes from the rocking gondolas and the occasional mournful cry from a seagull.

'Do you think there's anywhere open?' Rosemary asks. I pray that there is, as I'm desperate for a coffee and the bathroom; not necessarily in that order. I think we all are.

'It's Sunday, but we could be lucky,' Luciano says, doubtfully. But this is Venice. As we wander around while the dawn breaks, sure enough, the place is stirring. Somewhat subdued, we find the only cafe open and sit there with a cappuccino and cornetto, killing time before our *pensione* opens and the guys can finally check into a hotel.

Bidding our new friends goodbye and fortified by the hot refreshments, we are ready to front up to our *pensione* owner. Our host shakes her head before reluctantly letting us in.

She's a charmer.

We collapse on our beds and sleep for an hour or two before showering and getting dressed. At five to ten, we make our way down to reception. As we hand our key over, the host again shakes her head at us, clearly having come to her own conclusion about what we've been up to with the guys. Her disapproval doesn't stop her from taking our money, though.

I am sad to bid farewell to the sisters when we arrive back in Florence, but they have to return to Rome and their music course. The trip has been a distraction, a way of avoiding the thorny problem of my future and what to do next, and I feel very deflated after our Venetian adventure.

My time in Florence is coming to an end as the course finishes this month. What to do and where to go next? I don't yet know.

I can't say that I'm too sorry to be leaving Florence. Although I've had fun here, I've also hit rock bottom at times. The banking strike stunned me and having to ask for financial help on my own in a foreign country was terrifying. Without financial independence, my world was diminished and I couldn't think of anything else but getting through each day, worrying that I'd run out of money by the evening.

But despite everything, to go back to Australia now seems defeatist. I'm not done here in Italy and I need to find a way to move forward. My Italian is passable; I can get by day-to- day, but I'm not able to hold a conversation, nor can I understand anything but the simplest of jokes.

If I could get a live-in job, then I could keep practising the language. I apply for a few au pair jobs—half-heartedly, I have to admit. The only youngsters I've ever looked after were canine, equine and feline, and I've no experience (or enthusiasm) with little humans. Luckily for me, prospective employers come to the same conclusion.

A friend who lives in London suggests I come to England with her and find work there, generously offering me a place to stay while I find my feet. I desperately need money coming in, and as I have a British passport, there's no restriction on me being able to work. And England, where my sister lives, is the most sensible option open to me right now. I'd be a fool not to take my friend up on her offer.

We arrive in Dover on the ferry from Calais on a miserable late-December day. As we trudge from the ship to the boat train, me stopping every now and again to switch my heavy suitcase from one hand to the other, it sleets. This isn't exactly the grand arrival in England I've fantasised about.

A few days later, it's New Year's Eve. A little to my dismay, I end up going to a party full of Australians and New Zealanders, reminding me of all I want to leave behind for a while. Playing to the crowd, the DJ selects Men at Work's popular song of the time 'Down Under' and everyone leaps up and cheers as soon as they hear the familiar opening bars.

Everyone except me.

5

Fame!

London, 1983
Another popular song of the time is UB40's 'One in Ten,' written about the terrible level of unemployment in Britain in the 80s. Now I'm one of those unemployed, I feel like a fool for giving up my job back in Sydney. But in Australia, I tell myself, the economy isn't doing much better than it is in the UK.

I sign up with a temping agency in the City. This agency seems to prefer Antipodeans, saying we're hardworking compared with the usual applicants: the entitled Sloane Ranger rejects from the Lucie Clayton Charm Academy. On my 24th birthday, the agency sends me on an assignment to work in the back office of a major bank. It's not so much an office as a dungeon, I observe as I reach the airless basement where I'm expected to work. My job is to type columns of numbers and add them up with a calculator, putting in a running total of all the figures, and then trying but failing to make them all tally.

It's Best & Less all over again, the only difference being that I'm three years older. I feel like I've fallen down the snake when all I want to do is climb the ladder. My line manager stands over me getting more agitated by the minute, wisps of hair growing out of his bald head reminding me of an exasperated bird in full spring moult. By mid-afternoon on my first day, I can no longer stand the oppressive atmosphere. I mutter some excuse about feeling poorly, grab my bag and get out of there, taking the stairs to freedom two at a time.

Despite the desperate economy, low-paid work seems plentiful enough in London. As my fallback is waitressing, I apply to a vegetarian restaurant in Soho and am invited for an interview. A relic from the 1960s, the restaurant serves salads of beansprouts, carrot sticks, raw beets, celery and walnuts piled into tasteful pottery bowls, but this is radical compared with the rest of Britain in the 1980s where "salad" consists of iceberg lettuce, cucumber and tomatoes that taste of cotton wool, all dressed with plastic sachets of Heinz Salad Cream.

An apple-cheeked woman in her forties is head of recruitment. Her Aztec necklace over a plain pinafore dress is at odds with her clipped 1950s BBC radio announcer tones; I didn't know there was such a thing as a rich hippie. All the ones I've met have been poor.

A clipboard on her lap, she makes notes while I answer her questions, which are all fairly standard. But I notice that when she looks up, she glances at my hair; it's currently yellow rather than blonde with a bit of regrowth, which I've tried to disguise.

As we finish up the interview, she turns to me. 'Is that your natural hair colour? Because if it isn't, I'm afraid we can't employ you. Hair dye doesn't fit with our wholesome image.' I've been here before: another prospective employer making comments about my appearance. Only this time, all she's offering is part-time work that won't even cover half my London rent.

We're in Soho where every other young person channels Madonna or Boy George, and this woman wants her staff to look like Heidi?

'Yes, it is natural,' I lie. 'And it's a relief that you don't think I'm the right fit. I can't afford to work for the miserable wages you're offering.'

Mrs Smug's back stiffens. I doubt that it has even occurred to this woman how expensive rent is in London and that her staff might not have the money to pay their bills, let alone be able to afford to go to a hairdresser. But it is true that I need to do something about my hair before I attend any more interviews.

I walk everywhere in central London to save money, discovering what is to become a favourite route. After window-shopping at Liberty's, admiring its quirky jewellery and fashion, I cross Regent Street and wander up to Hanover Square, passing Vogue House and ending up in Fenwick's, the boutique department store on New Bond Street in Mayfair. At Brook Street, I walk towards South Molton Street, drifting into Browns to linger amongst clothes I can't afford. The opportunity to lap up the designer luxury in a glamourous part of London is too good to miss, so I pretend I belong there. And when scouts from Vidal Sassoon's Academy spot me as I peer into shop windows, I can't believe my luck.

I agree to become a hair model for demonstrations for both cutting and colouring, which costs me nothing. The supervisor is a leading hairdresser and he doesn't let a trainee go near my head without approving each snip or highlight. Even the trainees are all experienced hairdressers who have come here from all across the world for advanced training and to learn modern techniques. In return for giving up a day of my time, which breaks up the monotony of sending out job applications, I end up with a top West End cut and colour.

I step out of Sassoon's with an asymmetrical bob in shades of strawberry and vanilla, ready to conquer London. At Pineapple Dance Centre in Covent Garden, I fit right in and am hired as a receptionist on the spot.

I stroll down Floral Street on my first day in my new job and glance at the rehabilitation studio next door to Pineapple. There are dancers hanging from hooks on walls like giant fruit bats, and the rest are being put through their paces on what look like various implements of torture. When I ask what is going on, I'm told that it's a new therapy the dance centre is trying out to treat back injuries; it's called Pilates and is only available to injured dancers. This is years before Pilates becomes mainstream.

The dance centre is buzzing; it's so busy that the front desk needs three, sometimes four of us booking members in. On the odd occasion it's quiet, the other receptionists and I sing show tunes and play silly pranks on each other—it's the best fun I've had in ages.

But there is a catch, of course. I've yet to grasp the terrible wages in London compared with what I was earning in Sydney, and at the interview, I thought the amount offered was per day instead of per week. My first pay cheque comes as something of a nasty surprise.

After my first Sunday shift, which goes on until 10pm, I miss the last Tube home as the trains stop running early on Sunday nights. My only other viable option is the night bus, but I'm knackered so treat myself to a taxi back to Kilburn, leaving me with very little money to get me through the week. Because of the wages—or rather, the lack of them—I realise my time at Pineapple will be short-lived. But while I'm here, I'm determined to make the most of the free dance and exercise classes. And that's not the only perk of the job.

One morning, three scowling girls with no make-up on troop in. One of my colleagues nudges me as they walk straight past, noses in the air.

'Who are they?' I whisper once they've disappeared up the stairs. He leaps out from behind the desk and bursts into song, getting the dance moves to 'It Ain't What You Do, It's the Way That You Do It' spot on.

'Ahh,' I say, realisation dawning. 'Bananarama.' The other two receptionists, both ex-drama school, join him to sing harmony. Then the door opens and the boss walks in with someone I assume must be the group's manager. My colleagues' impromptu Bananarama tribute comes to an abrupt end as they dive back behind the reception desk and one grabs the booking sheet.

'They're in studio two,' he says, looking up with a beaming smile while trying to avoid eye contact with the boss's icy stare.

One of our jobs is to run up and down to the rehearsal studios, clearing away coffee cups and making sure the visiting stars have got everything they need. This allows us a sneak peek through the window to the studio; pretending to be checking on something or other, we enjoy a good gawp. Whether it's too early, they're hungover or have had a row, the Bananarama girls don't seem to be having a good day. The music for 'Cruel Summer' keeps stopping and starting as they fluff their routine again and again. The choreographer, brought in to teach them their dance moves, must have endless patience, but even he seems to be struggling as their rehearsal over-runs. And the crew from reception, me included, aren't helping, spying on them through the window and corpsing at every mistake.

Pineapple is in the beating heart of London's theatre land. If there was some sort of career structure here, I'd love to stay, but there's no way I can afford to. At least it makes it easier to get interviews for more permanent work when I can say that I'm currently employed.

6

This is Spinal Tap

On the strength of my previous experience in Australia, a start-up employs me to recruit researchers to write economic and political reports, similar to those published by the Economist Intelligence Unit. Once the company is up and running, my role will be to copy edit and proofread the documents before they're sent out to clients. I get to hand-pick the team I'll be working with as well as earn decent money, and there's a chance to grow with the company. It's too good an opportunity to turn down.

When I tell my new employers I want to move into a PR role once they're established, they seem happy. If I'm able to carve out a role for myself, that's fine by them. I've not only scored a salaried post, it's in swanky New Bond Street. A Monopoly fan as a kid, I've always loved the expensive real estate in the area. Not much has changed since my childhood. I make the leap from trade to TV not by answering newspaper advertisements, but by networking. Channel 4 Television has recently launched and commissions a raft of programmes from emerging filmmakers. For once, I'm in the right place at the right moment. I become friends with an investigative journalist who worked on the *Sunday Times* Insight team. Now a filmmaker, she becomes my mentor.

Without the helping hand of this sisterhood, I wouldn't have stood a chance. If I'd had to apply for a TV job advertised in a newspaper, I would have been knocked out in the initial round. There's nothing on paper that makes me stand out, unless a TV company needs an extra to make a white sauce without a recipe or ride a horse. As many of my new colleagues gained a first from Oxbridge, I keep quiet about my average degree and work for nothing for six weeks, while still having to pay for rent, bills, transport and food upfront.

In my new role, I transcribe audio tapes, help run the production office and learn to clear the rights to a ton of film and photo archive material for a six-part drama-documentary series about the British Empire. When I join, the office is in Covent Garden, near Soho, the coolest place in swinging London. Old Compton Street becomes a favourite haunt as it's one of the few places where I can buy decent take-away coffee. In the evenings, I meet up with friends and go to the basement at the Pollo Bar.

I'm still a hair model at Sassoon's Academy. Even though I now have a regular pay cheque, a West End cut and colour still costs more than I have left at the end of the week. And once you've had your hair done for free, it's a tough habit to give up. I have to take a half day off for each modelling session, but I make up for it by working late on other days.

The job certainly cannot be called boring. On a film shoot on top of Guy's Hospital, the tallest building in London at the time, I put my waitressing skills to the test, climbing up a metal ladder onto the roof while balancing a tray of coffees. Not a drop is spilt; I knew my random skills would come in handy one day. Another job involves trekking off to Chinatown to meet an expert calligrapher.

His task is to write an edict in Mandarin for a prop to use in a programme about the nineteenth century tea trade, and he transcribes the phrase I want him to write on a carefully prepared piece of parchment, which—appropriately—I've aged using cold tea. Unfortunately, he makes a mistake and, before I can stop him, dabs the parchment with liquid paper correction fluid. I have to dash back to the office, find another piece of parchment, repeat the ageing process and return to Chinatown for a second attempt.

Our office in Covent Garden is bursting at the seams, and after six months, the company moves us to the Rough Trade Records building in King's Cross. Our new premises are huge after the cramped room we all shared, but King's Cross is a wasteland compared with Covent Garden. There are no shops, and at lunchtime there is very little to do apart from wandering along the canals or popping up to Islington.

It's in this office that I first use a computer, a green-screen Amstrad. I don't like it at all and pine for my electric typewriter.

This technology will never fly.

I turn out to be wrong about that, don't I? And I am also wrong about a particular band, signed to Rough Trade, that uses the offices as a rehearsal space in the evenings. Working late one day, we are treated to the opening lines of a song depressingly entitled 'Heaven Knows I'm Miserable Now'. I liked the first two singles by The Smiths, 'Hand in Glove' and 'This Charming Man,' but this one sounds dire. We are so fed up with the din that we find some brooms, bang on the ceiling and yell for the band to be quiet.

'It'll never be a hit,' I shout.

I set up shoots, prepare budgets, organise editing, and am even roped in as an extra on set, but neither horse-riding nor white sauce is required. Posing as a 1980s yuppie, I have to wear a horrible brown skirt suit; I'm supposed to represent a young Margaret Thatcher look-alike. We film in a city branch of Marks & Spencer, the food hall being the favourite grocery shop for time-poor yuppies, as I pile expensive ready-meals for one and other aspirational foods such as mangos and avocados in my shopping basket.

Our office becomes a revolving door of friends of friends who went to university together. I don't know who half these people are, but they are keen to offer their opinion on how the drama-documentary series is shaping up. And one of them is Seán. He invites me to a party, but on this occasion, I can't go as I'm heading back to New Zealand to see Mum. However, our paths are destined to cross again when I return. So not only have I landed my first job in TV, I have also met my future husband.

After two and a half years as part of a small team working on a documentary series, I find it scary to have to look for employment again. Television jobs are mostly freelance and short-term, and to pay the bills, I need regular, reliable work.

An actor friend introduces me to a temping agency which specialises in placing administration staff in media jobs. After my disastrous experience temping in the City, it's a joy to be back in the West End. I even pass the typing test with my less than impressive 40wpm; how fast I type doesn't seem to matter.

'Do I have to dress up?' I ask the two women who run the agency.

'Good heavens, no,' they reply. 'What you've got on now is fine.' I'm wearing a circular skirt and a fifties top. They are the loveliest of employers—not only are they tolerant of my dress sense, but they are my financial saviours. As it can be lonely being the sole temp in an organisation, on Thursday afternoons, they invite those of us who aren't working that week in for a chat while we pick up our pay. On occasion, there's even wine. I've fallen on my feet once again.

One of my favourite placements is with a major record label in Marylebone, behind Oxford Street. I'm sent to work with various departments, including the promotions section of the Marketing Department, working for someone with the eye-catching name of Dawn Raid. I imagine police sirens, squealing brakes and burly coppers battering down doors, and love announcing in my telephone voice, 'Call for Dawn Raid on line 1.' I assume Dawn has given herself the coolest name ever, but no, her parents named her that. Did they give her brother a glorious name too? Midnight, perhaps? He might be plain old Dave.

As well as dishing out vinyl albums to journalists, I am tasked with the important job of listening to Radio 1 and scanning the playlists, noting how many times a day the label's artists are given airtime. As soon as one of "our" artists comes on, I run into the Artists and Repertoire room and announce stuff like, 'Alright, let's make some noise for… (insert artist's name here).' Unfortunately, during the morning in A&R, most of the seats are empty, and those who have made it in before lunchtime are always nursing hangovers.

A&R appears to be the cushiest job in the record industry, so naturally, the only way in is to be a bloke. It might be a classless department – the 'OK, ya' of Chas and Guy mingles with the 'Alright, mate' of Terry and Tony – but it sure is sexist. Life expectancy in A&R is short; these people are lucky they aren't deaf by thirty after too many late-night gigs with music so loud, they need ear-defenders. And once they settle down and have kids, they're considered too old to stay out all night, so get replaced by younger and cheaper single men.

Another of my tasks is to keep the aspiring hopefuls (aka emerging bands) at bay. They don't give up, bombarding us with flyers about upcoming gigs, followed by pleading phone calls. It doesn't help that there's a TV ad running where a band is playing on the street outside a record company. The staff, hearing this great new music, stop what they're doing, open the windows, and cheer and clap. A bunch of lads must have mistaken the ad for real life as they do, in fact, perform an impromptu gig outside our offices. But sadly for them, it's the morning so nobody from A&R is here to see them.

How bands ever get to break through is a mystery to me. There's no point sending in an unsolicited demo tape as the A&R guys receive a mountain of those in the post. If they ever get around to opening all this mail, they then ask me to plonk the tapes on the desk of the guy who is meant to listen to them.

'If the bands were any good, we'd know who they are by now,' he complains without fail. After a week of his grumbling, I cut out the middle-man and chuck the tapes straight in the bin.

After dark, the rock-and-roll lifestyle is fuelled by stronger stuff than PG Tips, but even rockers like their old-fashioned home comforts. By 3pm, we're all flagging and there's nothing nicer than the lift doors opening and the tea lady wheeling out a trolley laden down with a tea urn and medicinal Kit-Kats. My duties include answering the phone, which means I work up a thirst for my daily cuppa, and sending out albums to music journalists who request them.

Most of the artists and bands are too mainstream for my tastes, except for a jazz label that manages the back catalogue of artists like Josephine Baker. I decide that a former listings journalist of my acquaintance is a worthy recipient for an entire stack of albums from this label. It just so happens that we share a home address, so I send them to his workplace. Not that anyone in the profligate 1980s would care.

A few free albums dished out here and there is nothing compared with what's coming next. I'm hired for three weeks over the summer to be the gatekeeper of the office of the finance boss, except the man in question has bolted. As has a seven-figure sum of money. Allegedly. One rumour flying around the company is that he was last seen heading for the south of France and that the police are keen to talk to him to "assist with their enquiries." Another theory is that he absconded with the petty cash. In the record biz, "petty cash" doesn't mean coinage to buy a round of coffees; it's a catch-all phrase for the eye-watering expenses that rock stars run up while recording an album, or for paying off the various late-night parasites that the A&R team encounter in their vital work of going to the gigs of up-and-coming bands in their quest to be the one to sign the next U2.

It turns out I have been hired to keep up appearances; all I have to do is sit at his desk, look important, answer his phone and take messages. If anyone asks where he is, I give a different answer each time.

'He's on holiday.' 'Off sick.'

'How should I know? I'm only the temp.'

So far, the management have kept the allegations against the missing man a secret, but it can't be long before the press gets hold of the story, so I'm wary of outside calls.

Anyone who I suspect might be a journalist, I refer on to the Press Officer.

After three days of excitement and speculation, the fuss dies down and the phone stops ringing. I am left with nothing to do officially—for twelve whole days. So I spring into action and get on with my side hustle: producing a short film. In an office the size of a tennis court, I busy myself by writing up budgets, creating call sheets and schedules, making maps, organising the crew, and booking edits. I run backwards and forwards to the printer as I have twenty copies of scripts to produce, and the massive desk I sit at is incredibly useful for running my pop-up production office. The record company is so laid back in general that it must appear odd to anyone walking past how efficient I am. But although we are less than a mile from 221B Baker Street, not one aspiring Holmes or Watson so much as pokes their head around the door to enquire what exactly is going on here.

Not only am I furthering my film and TV career, I'm being paid for doing so. I have no line manager to report to, just a time sheet to fill in at the end of the week, which is never queried. I have no qualms about that; as long as I arrive and leave at the correct time, no one cares.

After television, the music industry seems superficial. It's not as if I get to spot any rock stars. Even when my best friend from boarding school, who works in a rather more glamorous role in the industry, takes me as her VIP guest to Live Aid, it isn't enough to convince me the record industry is where it's at.

Mind you, as my brief encounter with Bananarama proves, I'm not ever so good at recognising famous people when I do meet them. At Wembley Stadium, my friend and I get into a lift along with a shortish grey-haired man, and while the other women in the lift nudge each other and look sidelong at him, I mouth to her, 'Who is he?' The man grins. I think he can lip read.

As we exit the lift and he walks off, my friend whispers in disbelief, 'That was only Richard Gere.'

Now I've failed to spot a famous Hollywood movie star.

No wonder he thought it was funny that I didn't know who he was.

7

The Da Vinci Code

I'm told on Friday that the following Monday, I will be not only back in Bond Street, one of my favourite haunts, but at Sotheby's, the auction house for the seriously loaded. And I'll be working for Lord Westmorland—a peer of the realm! I spend the entire weekend practising my curtseying and walking out of rooms backwards.

By Sunday night, I've got the patter right: 'Yes, M'Lud; No, Your Lordship; I'll have that typed out in ten minutes, sir.' As online search engines don't exist at the time, nor do I have a print copy of *Burke's Peerage*, I'm unable to look him up. But I do discover that his other job title is Master of the Horse and nearly faint on the spot. We have horses in common! I wonder if he likes white sauce, too…

The Master of the Horse, according to Wikipedia, is now mainly a ceremonial role held by a hereditary peer. In former times, the holder played an important role in the sovereign's household. A big cheese, then; I had to get that backing out of the room thing spot on.

On the Monday morning in question, I stand outside 34-35 New Bond Street W1 and glance up. The building is late

Georgian and above the entrance is an ancient statue of the Egyptian lion-goddess, Sekhmet. If it's this grand on the outside, what's it going to be like on the inside? Sadly, I don't get to find out; I'm spirited away from the grand foyer and guided towards the side entrance.

As I trudge up the narrow stairs to the fifth floor in what must have once been a private house, I realise I'm off to where the Georgian servants lived. It reminds me of going to the opera in Barcelona, bypassing the grandeur and sitting in the cheap seats up with the gods. At least an attic in the West End is a cut above a basement in the City.

The Duke—or rather, Barry, as he insists I call him—greets me. He reminds me of a history professor; I picture him driving a clapped-out Volvo Estate that smells of wet Labrador. It's boiling hot in the attic as there is only a tiny window and it's summer. But it's more like a small flat than an office, complete with a sink and a kettle. The two rooms are filled with books, making it very cosy. But where are the paintings and the sculptures? I feel very far removed from the rarefied atmosphere of fine-art auctions.

Sotheby's is a crusty but venerated institution, at the time yet to be tainted by scandals relating to price fixing, art forgery and alleged stolen goods. As we sit down with a cup of coffee, Barry tells me he contracted me to work on a recipe book that Sotheby's will be publishing. He wants me to type it from handwritten notes, and then proofread it. As jobs go, this seems pleasant enough. I can work at my own pace. And I might even try out some of the recipes.

The first challenge is to decipher the handwriting. It is bold and slopes on an angle to the right, and the recipes are written in fountain pen so there are blots on the page. The content doesn't exactly scream bestseller. The author has a passion for what to do with left-overs—or rather, her cook does—as I count at least twenty ways to make rissoles. Some Duchess wrote it—Argyle? Devonshire? Alice's Wonderland? I'm not sure which—and it has all the appearances of a vanity project.

Why are we bothering with this?

In answer to my unspoken question, Barry assures me that it's because the Duchess of Cloud Cuckoo Land is paying most of our wages. I'm glad we get that out of the way.

The only visible clue to Barry's status is that he lunches at Claridge's, a five-minute walk from New Bond Street on the corner of Brook Street and Davies Street in Mayfair. When I'm asked to go down there and interrupt him in the middle of lunch to sign papers, I have never been so over-awed by my surroundings. It would take me another thirty years before I'd cross that threshold again, this time as a customer. And that will only be because I've got caught in a rainstorm and the friend I am with recommends a drink in the bar.

* * *

A regular placement for me is with a television station based in Euston Road. I'm hired for a week to fill in as the Duty Officer, working a late shift and finishing at 10pm. This role involves fielding phone calls from viewers who ring in to express their opinions about the programmes that have been on that evening. A colleague reassures me that it's easy, with a dozen calls a night if I'm lucky. On my first shift, Channel 4 broadcasts its new comedy-drama series *Teachers* and the switchboard is jammed all night. And this is only episode one.

The premise is that teachers are as unruly (if not worse)

than their students. Favourite locations are the pub, where the teachers fall over drunk, and behind the bike sheds where they are caught smoking. It's not the first time the teaching profession has been satirised, but the nation clearly isn't amused as the broadcast triggers an onslaught of abuse—viewers aren't shy in expressing their disgust. I talk to retired teachers, current teachers, parents of teachers and head teachers, holding the phone at arm's length to protect my ears from all the shouting.

Why didn't I think this through before I took this job? Nobody's going to ring in and say they like a programme, are they?

I can't remember how many calls I log. My right hand seizes up; I can barely keep pace. I keep my notes brief, recording the caller's name and whether the comment is negative or positive—I can count on one hand the number of positive comments. Who will read them, anyway?

Once the furore dies down, the following night is relatively quiet, although the calls are more serious as they're from drunks, the lonely and the suicidal. I don't know why viewers in distress ring the Duty Office; maybe it's because they know somebody will be there to take their call. As I listen to the sob stories before referring the callers on to dedicated helplines such as the Samaritans, I also deal with calls about programmes broadcast by a rival that has its own dedicated Duty Office. It's pointless to refer the callers on, as all this does is make them angrier. They need to vent and don't care to whom. And tonight, that's me.

On and off, I spend six months temping as an Administrative Assistant at the TV station while trying to get freelance production television work. It's rare that I get sent to production departments, but I jump at the once-in-a-lifetime opportunity of one particular assignment. I'm contracted to help the Production Assistant during the filming of Sir Michael Tippett's opera, *The Midsummer Marriage*. It's a one-off big-budget production directed by Elijah Moshinsky.

I'm on a high. I observe acting royalty, as the Director has carved out a non-singing cameo role for none other than Dame Janet Suzman. Not only is this my chance to work in prestige drama, it's an opportunity to gain experience of working on an opera for television.

While the Production Assistant plans each day's filming, breaking down the script into portions in order to record the music and the vocals, I type out the call sheets. We're shooting down at Teddington, beside the Thames. It takes me an hour to get there by train every morning, so it does feel like we're on location, far away from central London.

Now that I have a taste for drama, this is all I want to do. But in the meantime, I need to pay the bills. As I walk up the long escalator at Warren Street Tube station and cross Euston Road to the TV company's London HQ after my fun time "on location," I come crashing back to earth when I'm sent to work with a small team in Factual Television, commissioning a series of short documentaries by emerging filmmakers even younger than me. I should be more enthusiastic than I actually am, but I'm frustrated; I already have a six-part drama-documentary series on my CV, but now I'm a lowly temp and it feels like I'm going backwards. Deciding I should forget the mainstream broadcasters that seem to be far too hierarchical, I redouble my efforts and send out a mailshot to as many independent production companies as I can find. All it takes is for one company to say yes, I tell myself.

One wet afternoon in April, as the rain drips down the inside of the sash window in the Vauxhall flat that Seán and

I have moved into together, the phone rings when I'm ironing while watching the Grand National. It's only the Producer of the *Comic Strip* (a franchise that makes films featuring leading comedy actors such as Dawn French, Jennifer Saunders, Adrian Edmondson and Rik Mayall), looking for a Production Coordinator. Do I want to come in for a little chat? My mouth opens and closes like a goldfish before I get so much as a word out.

How on earth did they find me?

'Seven hundred and fifty pounds a week alright for you, darling? It's an eight-week shoot.'

'Yes, that's great,' I gabble. I've never been offered that much money. By the end of the summer, I'll be six thousand quid richer. Unfortunately, I have a habit which my late father called "counting your chickens before they're hatched."

Sorry, Dad, I still do this.

'What's the film?' I ask.

'You'll love it. It's set in Wales and called *Strike*. I'll call you back, luvvy, to fix up a time for you to come and see us in Soho.'

I've scored an interview for a job I didn't even apply for. If I impress the interview panel, I'll be working on an actual film. No matter that it will be my first job as Production Coordinator; everyone has to start somewhere. And I worked on that opera, even if it was as Assistant to the Production Assistant.

I waltz around the room, pulling my clothes off the hangers in the wardrobe and trying on interview outfits. The Producer rings me just as I'm flinging off the fifth ensemble.

'Sorry, luvvy, no can do, I'm afraid,' which is producer

speak for "we've already found someone else we like better and were only sizing you up as a substitute."

Why build my hopes up like that when he'd offered it to another coordinator first?

The horse I'd backed in the National wins the race, but does so without a rider. It's not meant to be my day.

Of all the projects that got away, this is the one that rankles the most. *Strike* is a spoof action thriller about a former coal miner who pitches a serious script about the miners' strike to Hollywood. But of course, there's a twist, which sees Al Pacino cast as the union leader and Meryl Streep as his wife. In true *Comic Strip* style, Al Pacino is played by Peter Richardson and Meryl Streep by Jennifer Saunders. And just my luck, *Strike* becomes the best received *Comic Strip* film of all time—not only top-rated by the critics, but an audience favourite.

8

Halfway to Paradise

Glasgow, 1988
In the spring, I apply for a job on a contemporary popular culture magazine series, *Halfway to Paradise*, filming in Glasgow. The first of its kind to be made north of the border, the show will fill Channel 4's coveted 11.15 Friday-night national youth TV slot.

I don't mention my Sassenach (English) heritage and talk up my Celtic connections. As far as the two Scottish producers are concerned, I'm from South Island, New Zealand— Scotland Down Under. As Seán is known to one of them, this gives me an advantage. They hire me on a three- month contract and I am now an honorary Scot.

Full of excitement, I catch the Glasgow train from Euston. It's the height of summer in London, but in Glasgow, it feels more like autumn. I rent a room from an academic contact at the University who rattles around on his own in a large Victorian house in the West End, but I'm not intending to spend much time at my digs because of all the travelling involved in making the series. At weekends, I will fly home to London.

Halfway to Paradise features a mixture of live bands in the studio and filmed inserts about art, cinema, comedy, music and photography. The short inserts showcase the best of Scottish and Northern Irish film-school talent and are very popular with the targeted audience, who are culturally literate 18–35-year-olds. It's presented by "Mr Sinclair," a fictional 1950s bingo caller played by a stand-up comedian, who pretends to be out of touch with popular culture.

In Trevor Johnstone's review in *The List*, Issue 78, published on 30 September 1988, he praises the first episode:

'An impressive film on Glasgow photographer Oscar Marzaroli (which I worked on) sits side by side with an unashamedly emotive vignette starring a certain middle-aged mum who cuts a slushy ballad in a DIY recording studio. All this and vintage porridge adverts too (my bit!) makes for a remarkably flavoursome hour loosely organised around the theme of Gael culture.' The reviewer misses the point in his "an unashamedly emotive vignette" comment as it's a film of Jimmy Somerville's mum, who has a gravelly, tuneless singing voice, trying to record her son's hit song "Don't Leave Me This Way." What everyone wants to know after seeing the clip is, where did he get that beautiful voice? Not off his mum, that's for sure.

The series is a bold and brave project, but like any television trying to break new ground, it has its flaws, the main one being that the middle-aged presenter fails to engage the core audience. And it feels like it's trying too hard to be all things to all people. But it's worth watching for the live bands alone: as well as one of the first ever television performances by The Proclaimers, the series features the biggest Scottish names in independent music, from stadium rockers Simple Minds, Big Country, Texas and

Deacon Blue to Fairground Attraction and The Communards.

As both a Production Assistant and Film Archive Researcher, I spend many a happy hour down at the Scottish Screen Archive, finding amusing clips about representations of the country and its culture. It's my first time working in youth television, and with such a large production team. In Documentaries, there were four of us in the office. We hired in film crews for shoots as and when we needed them, but working this way meant it took three years to make one series. The trend now is to employ a large team on short-term contracts and get the programme or series made as fast as possible.

I'm proud of this series and it goes down well in Scotland. Even mainstream audiences, who might not have seen it yet, have heard of it. In England, it's a different story: 'Sorry, never heard of it' is something I hear regularly back in London. And that's the frustrating part. When I'm pitching for other production jobs, nobody who interviews me has seen the work I have done north of the border, despite the fact the series was broadcast across Britain.

The studio is at Parkhead Cross in the deprived East End of town, close to Celtic Football Club. Football is a religion up here; the rivalry between the two major Glasgow clubs is legendary. That much I know, but something as simple as sourcing sustenance is proving rather more difficult to grasp.

At lunchtime, I make my way to the local sandwich bars, trying to find something other than slices of white bread with orange cheese in between them.

'Could I have a bit of green salad in my sandwich?' I venture when the cheerful lady behind the counter asks me what I want. The other customers can't keep the astonishment off their faces as they grab the nearest orange cheese sandwich and shake their heads in a "wisht your blether, you soft Sassenach" way.

'Och, hen, we've nae green salad here,' she snorts as she passes over a cling-filmed package, a big smile on her face. Orange cheese it is, then.

After working late one evening, passing one of the best chip shops in town, I immediately fancy fish and chips for dinner. Lining up in the queue, I pay no attention to what the customers in front of me say when they order, so when my turn comes, I am totally unprepared.

'Fish and chips, please,' I say clearly. The woman behind the counter can't keep a straight face, and there's a spontaneous snort and giggle from the line behind me.

What have I done now?

'You'll be wanting a fish supper. Cod or haddock?' says the server.

I whisper, 'Haddock.' After she hands me the steaming hot package, I slink off, berating myself for yet another stupid faux pas.

One perk of the job is that at weekends, we can use the production cars if we pay for our own fuel. I duly book one well in advance of Seán's birthday weekend, which we have planned to spend in the English Lake District. Leaving work promptly at 5.30pm on the Friday, I'm stuck for the first hour crawling through rush-hour traffic, trying to get out of the city and on to the A74 south. The city roads all look the same; even though I'm going at under ten miles an hour, I have to concentrate. I don't dare even put the car radio on until I'm well on my way.

Although it's only the second week of September and it was still light when I set off, by the time I reach the M6, the sky is indigo and it's raining. But it isn't just any old rain; it is Lake District rain, coming at me horizontally. The car, a latest model Vauxhall Astra, has a decent set of windscreen wipers, but even they're no match for the water flying up from the spray of nose-to-tail motorway traffic.

I focus on the tail lights of the car in front. Trying my best to keep up with the traffic, I'm distracted by all the condensation building up in the car and the rear demister not working properly. Suddenly, a huge lorry with its lights flashing comes roaring up behind me. The driver blasts his horn, but there's nowhere for me to go. I've never driven alone on an unfamiliar motorway at night, let alone in these appalling road conditions, and now I'm so spooked, I imagine every driver is out to get me. I work myself up into such a state, I'm too scared to think to pull into the next set of motorway services and calm myself down.

Get a grip.

Once I reach the turnoff for Ambleside, I leave the mayhem behind and am on a country road. But it's dark and unlit, and I can't see the printed paper maps that tell me how to get from the motorway to Oxenholme Station. Luckily, the A684 for Kendal is well-signposted. I remember I need to turn left down a smaller road, then turn right to get to the station. But there's a car on my tail, and there's nowhere to pull over. Worse still, when I reach the junction, the left turn takes me into what isn't a road; it's a lane. What if I'm wrong and end up at a farm instead of a station? And if it is there, why is the whereabouts of the station such a secret? A signpost or two would be nice.

I sail past the turn and end up in Kendal. After driving around in endless circles, going nowhere, I finally spot the elusive sign for the railway station. I arrive just in time to meet Seán, beating the London train by two minutes.

We've booked a bed and breakfast close to Beatrix Potter's house in Near Sawrey. What a bargain; it's so perfect, I can hardly believe my luck. It's even close to a riding school, where I have a ride booked for the next day. By the time we get there, it's past 9pm. As our friendly host greets us, she suggests we drop our bags and make a dash for the pub to grab something to eat. We gladly follow her suggestion, and the pub is everything we could have wished for: warm, cosy and welcoming with an open fire and decent food.

The next morning, we open the curtains to our room—or rather, suite—to see that it looks out on to a large garden. There's a man of around thirty out there, pulling weeds out of the flowerbeds, then forking them over.

'This is a real find,' I say as we make our way to the farmhouse kitchen for breakfast. Laid out on the table is a bowl of fruit, a jug of juice and some homemade muesli, which we help ourselves to. Our host offers us a cooked full English breakfast, with local eggs and home-made preserves. As we linger over our coffee, the man we'd seen in the garden earlier comes in, nods to us, helps himself to some tea and goes out again.

At 11.30am, I wander up to the next village in my riding gear. There, waiting for me, is my horse, already tacked up. We're going for a hack beside Esthwaite Water, the nearest lake. I look between the pricked ears of my sturdy mount as the six of us clatter off. This little horse seems to want to be at the front, so I ride next to the lead instructor and we enjoy some chitchat.

'Are you staying nearby?' she enquires.

'We are. I found a good value B&B in Near Sawrey.' 'Oh, which one?'

I name the farmhouse where we're staying. 'We've got a self-contained room which is huge as well as our own bathroom. All that for forty quid a night. And our host cooked us a brilliant breakfast this morning.'

She turns to me, frowning. 'No one blames her,' she says.

This is cryptic.

'Is there something I should know?' I say, apprehensively.

'I don't want to spoil your holiday.'

You just did.

'We're only staying one more night. And she's been great so far.' I want to put my fingers in my ears and go, 'La, la, la, la.'

'You don't need to worry about her. But I'd be careful of her son.'

'We didn't see anyone else there when we arrived last night. And this morning, there was just the gardener, digging away. He came into the house for some tea, nodded and went out again.'

My riding companion turns towards me.

'That's him. He lives with her now, since he got let out of prison.'

'What did he do?' I try to think up some examples of heinous crimes. I get as far as armed robbery and GBH before she replies.

'He killed someone.'

It's lucky we're walking slowly, giving the horses a neck stretch on a long rein; if we were going any faster, I swear I'd have fallen off.

'I'm grateful you told me,' I say. 'And you haven't spoilt our weekend,' I lie.

She turns to me again, looking visibly relieved. 'You fancy a canter?'

'Yes, let's.' Generally, I'd always canter a horse in the school before doing so out on a hack, but as it appears I've booked the Bates Motel for Seán's birthday treat, what more have I got to lose?

* * *

That night, after another fine meal in the pub, we arrive back at the B&B, lock our bedroom door and put a chair underneath its handle. We have our own bathroom—we don't have to venture beyond our room in the night. I vow to stay up, listening out for every creak in the floorboards, but all that country air knocks me out cold. Mother and son could have been re-enacting the infamous shower scene from *Psycho*, for all I know.

On Sunday morning, there's no sign of the son at breakfast.

Maybe he's at church, atoning for his sins?

We pack the car, pay up, thank our host, and drive off. I stop at the bottom of the driveway, and in my rear-view mirror, I see him in the garden, staring at us. Did we ever see mother and son together at the same time? My mind conjuring up an image of the man dressed in his mother's clothes and carrying a large knife, I'm glad to be out of there.

We fit in a couple of hours' walking before having to part company again for the working week. As I drop Seán at Oxenholme and head back on the drive to Glasgow, I think about my journey down on Friday night in the rain and the dark. And how grateful I was when we arrived at the bed and breakfast. If it wasn't for that conversation on my ride, I'd have been none the wiser. Maybe next time, I'll be more careful about booking a so-called "bargain holiday"; there's usually a reason something is cheap.

* * *

Although I miss Seán during the week, work is very sociable as most of the team, like me, are living away from home. Apart from one who is a single parent, the rest of us regularly go out for drinks and dinner to avoid going back to rented digs.

When the series comes to a close, I'm one of the last to leave as my colleagues head home. No longer having a midweek social life, I spend my evenings back at my digs. Logan is a friendly host, but we keep very much to ourselves, apart from late in the evenings. He'll often still be up, sitting in the living room, a bottle of single malt whisky beside him. He generally invites me to join him for a wee dram and, as I enjoy his company, I say yes. I'm surprised how mellow the whisky is on the back of my throat, but one is enough for me; two at most if the conversation's flowing. When I get up and turn in for the night, I leave him there, drinking on his own.

The next morning, there's another empty bottle on the kitchen counter.

As the weeks wear on, I realise Logan has a serious drinking problem. And if he carries on, that the booze will probably kill him. I feel sad for his girlfriend; she's a lovely person and she must see it, too. But even if she tries to help him, an addict has to have a reason to give up. And Logan never seems like he does.

Sadly, my worst fears for this gentle and likeable man with a big problem weighing him down are realised. He dies a few years later of an alcohol-related health condition. While it's a sociable way of unwinding for many of us, the sad truth is that drinking can turn into something far more sinister when the fun stops and it becomes an addiction.

9

Welcome to Sweden

As it turns out, my landlord in Glasgow isn't going to be the only alcoholic I have to deal with in 1988. After returning from Scotland, I'm preoccupied with finding somewhere to live. When the educational charity Seán works for closes down, we are both in insecure employment; the best we can manage between us is Seán's two part-time lectureship jobs and my short-term freelance TV contracts, interspersed with temping. Our chances of getting on the property ladder seem to be diminishing by the hour.

But this is the financially deregulated 1980s, an era of liar loans and banks happy to keep their clients in debt for the next thirty years. And as I have a decent deposit from the sale of a property I bought with a friend, a building society takes pity on us. Unfortunately, though, since the US stock market crashed by 20% on 19 October 1987, a day dubbed Black Monday, interest rates have been rising. Soon, they soar to 17% and we struggle to pay the mortgage on our modest two-bedroom maisonette in Stoke Newington.

Now that we have rapidly growing mortgage repayments to consider, temping week to week becomes increasingly precarious as it often means gaps when I don't have an income. A weight lifts from my shoulders when I'm contracted for six months as a Production Secretary to a recently launched Swedish TV station located in Camden. This is yet another demotion, but for now, I set my ambitions aside, at least until the mortgage rates drop.

With this in mind, I have turned down the second series of *Halfway to Paradise* as it was only a three-month contract and I would have rent to pay on top of an expensive mortgage. Something had to give, and that was to be my weekly commute to the other end of Britain. If I'd been offered a promotion, I'd have said yes, but it was the same job as before. I wasn't going to be learning anything new, so it wasn't worth making the personal and financial sacrifice of being away from home.

Talking of being far from home, I feel for my new boss who has moved to London from his home in Stockholm, leaving his wife and young family behind. He has a haunted, harried expression and seems ill at ease from the very first week. The job he's taken on seems to be stressing him out and the company has barely started. For my part, I struggle to keep up with his list of demands.

My colleagues are mostly Swedes, with a handful of Danes and Norwegians. The Norwegians remind me of New Zealanders, while the Swedes are aloof initially, but it doesn't take long for the ice to break. My colleagues think of London as a fun town and are looking to me as their local guide for the best places to party.

We start out with drinks after work, which lead on to dinner. And then we mark birthdays by going out at lunchtimes. Each occasion involves wine. Bottles and bottles of it. My colleagues are amazed at how cheap alcohol is in London compared with Scandinavia.

Unfortunately, easy access to booze proves to be my boss's downfall. But he never joins us on our outings; he does his drinking alone, which is far more dangerous. Most mornings, he comes in late, until one day he doesn't appear at all. I hear on the grapevine that the company has sent him home to Sweden to dry out. I hope for his family's sake, he succeeds.

* * *

Launched in 1988, my employer is the first pan-Scandinavian commercial television station to broadcast to Denmark, Norway and Sweden. Based in London to avoid the strict Swedish broadcasting legislation that bans advertiser-supported television, it uplinks its programmes via satellite. We even plan to make a feature of the new satellite service we are switching to in 1989.

We record the live launch in December 1988. It's a big deal as several other broadcasters, including MTV Europe and Sky TV, will be making the switch. In the studio before dawn to record the live satellite launch from French Guiana in South America, I will provide precise timings to the director in the control room while our presenter in the studio provides commentary in Swedish, a language I neither speak nor understand. The company that owns the satellite will broadcast in French.

This is my baptism of fire in live television, and only the second time I've worked as a Production Assistant in a television studio control room. As I start the countdown—'Ten, nine, eight'—I hear my voice quaking and I feel sick to the stomach.

Don't screw this up.

How hard can it be to time each segment and make sure

we're following the script? Not difficult at all—if only I spoke Swedish. At least I understand the facts and figures to do with the rocket: cost (millions); weight (1,768 kg). The presenter gives some background to the launch site: being close to the equator means that the spacecraft uses up less energy to get into orbit. Or at least, I hope that's what he is saying as that's what we discussed in the meeting yesterday. If he misses something out, the director—a fierce woman at the best of time—will shout me into next week.

As the vision mixer cuts from the presenter to the live link of the rocket about to blast off into space, I'm slightly less scared after ten minutes of abject terror. The rocket fires up its engines and the cool-as-a-cucumber scientist begins the countdown at the launch site:

'*Dix, neuf, huit…*'
Glad I'm not the one having to do it.

Because this is to be broadcast to a family audience, in his interesting facts and figures about the space centre in Kourou, the presenter has been primed to avoid the 'in an unlikely event of an accident' scenario by omitting to say that the site has been chosen as it's near the sea to minimise the number of human casualties from the debris of a launch failure. There's a lot of money riding on this rocket. Luckily, everything goes without a hitch as we have lift off.

We high five each other in the gallery before the vision mixer switches back to the studio and the presenter wraps up. It feels like we've done a day's work and it's only 6am.

It's going to be a long day.

10

A Hard Day's Night

Littleborough, 1989
In the autumn of 1989, Seán is offered a full-time post at Liverpool John Moores University. To misquote a Tory minister, he did indeed 'Get on his bike and look for work,' and he kept looking until he found it. A permanent move out of London is a big deal as we are the first of our friends to leave. But the only way we're going to make any headway on paying off our mortgage is to sell up in London and move north, where housing is half the price.

I've filmed in the North East, Yorkshire and Scotland. And everyone has been so friendly in the north; they call me "pet" or "hen". What's not to like? I haven't actually been to Liverpool since the 1960s when my family caught a passenger ship to Malaysia, and all I remember is that it was freezing cold and pelting with rain as we waited to board at the docks. I imagine it's changed a bit since then —it's the home of the Beatles, there's a new Tate Gallery and *This Morning* is broadcast from the Albert Dock. I reckon I'll be fine, even though the weather is probably the same. I'm so confident, I don't even bother to accompany Seán up there for a recce when he goes for his interview.

When we first move, we live closer to Manchester than Liverpool because several national and regional TV production companies are based there. The only major Liverpool production company is Mersey Television, which makes the soap *Brookside*. As I have no experience in series drama, I'm doubtful they'd hire me. We find an old weaver's cottage in the little hamlet of Summit in Littleborough and sign up for a six-month lease while we look around for somewhere more permanent.

At first, I treat it as a holiday escape to the countryside. In two minutes, we can be out of the house and down at the Rochdale Canal. A pair of graceful swans glide up and down, and the only other living creatures we encounter on our walk are the inquisitive sheep grazing in the nearby hills. What a contrast to the urban canal paths of north London, where you have to try not to fall into the water while dodging the ninja cyclists who tear along them. Further east in the Calder Valley are Hebden Bridge and Heptonstall. We explore the area to immerse ourselves in nature and the region's rich literary history, treading the same paths that the Bronte sisters, Ted Hughes and Sylvia Plath once walked.

Our local shops are in Todmorden, a town four miles away which we cycle to on the towpath. It has a brilliant health food shop run by three flame-haired sirens, so we go vegetarian for a bit, and then Seán becomes vegan in an attempt to give up smoking. When it doesn't cure his addiction, he abandons it.

While I wait to hear from various TV companies, I return to working in restaurants. But instead of waiting tables, I graduate to the kitchen. An inn in Uppermill takes me on as a trainee chef while I study for a professional cooking qualification—not a fancy Cordon Bleu diploma, but a humble City and Guilds certificate at the local technical college, which I do on my two nights off from the restaurant. I learn to chop an onion so that it doesn't make me cry and how not to cut off my fingers while preparing other vegetables; how to joint a chicken and make hot water pastry. I glean a few tricks from the French family who run the pub; they teach me how to prepare French classics including celeriac remoulade and tarte aux pommes.

But the hours are relentless. I work split shifts, from 9.30am until 2.30pm, and then from 4.30pm until 10.30pm, five days a week from Wednesday to Sunday. When our lease is up for renewal, I still don't have a TV job. We decide that our future doesn't lie in the Pennines and head west to Oxton on the Wirral, four miles from Liverpool sitting on the other side of the Mersey.

* * *

The Wirral, 1990
Now I've left the Big Smoke and there is no media temping agency to fall back on, I accept another hospitality job, this time much closer to home at a tiny fine-dining restaurant in Oxton. The restaurant needs a pastry chef, but can't afford to pay the going rate, so hires me instead. I don't want to become a sous chef because of my allergy to, of all things, smoked salmon; this became apparent after I'd been preparing sixty-plus portions night after night in the Pennines.

Because the restaurant serves only twenty covers a day, I get away with my less-than-perfect plating skills while improving my baking. All diners are offered a selection of complementary homemade bread rolls with their dinner. I also learn everything I can from the chef, whose ambition I admire. He is in thrall to top London chef Marco Pierre White, trying to emulate him at every opportunity. But I feel sorry for this young chef; he's undoubtedly talented, but he doesn't know how to find investors willing to provide him with a much-needed injection of cash to allow him to stay afloat. When his lease comes up for renewal, he is forced to close the restaurant.

Still yearning for a career in television, I resort to sending out a mailshot of my CV to every production company in the North West, and in the interim, I answer an ad for market researchers. After going on a training course for a couple of companies, I pass and am given the job. This involves travelling to grey northern town centres to approach targeted consumers or door knocking on row upon row of houses. The surveys I dread most are in the leafy middle-class suburbs, where the houses are detached and far from each other, sitting proudly at the end of long driveways. Often, the posher the house, the ruder the reception.

Before I knock at a door, I do a quick scan of the house front. If the garden's unkempt or the curtains are closed, I move on. My spiel is ready in case I need to make an instant decision about my personal safety, the one thing our training didn't cover. When a man I don't like the look of answers the door and there's no sound of anyone else in the house, I tell him the survey is about washing powder before enquiring if there are any women at home. The lewd comments I often get in response demonstrate that my gut instinct is right and I feel vindicated in getting away from the door as fast as I can.

Of course, some people I meet in the line of my work are

lovely, if occasionally a little eccentric. One elderly lady takes pity on me on a wet afternoon and invites me in for a cup of tea, surprising me by asking if I'd like to meet her dog.

'It's a very well-behaved dog. It didn't bark when I knocked,' I say.

'He,' the lady corrects, tilting her head like Princess Di as she smiles. I guess her to be retired as she's at home in the daytime, so I shouldn't even be talking to her—retirees and the unemployed aren't proper consumers, according to my employers. It's shoppers with disposable income that matter as advertising influences their decisions about which product to buy. But because I'm weary and cold and love dogs, I accept her kind offer of tea.

'Here he is,' the lady says as we walk into the sitting room. There, in pride of place next to the television, is the most enormous display case containing a stuffed standard poodle with a glossy curly coat and glass eyes. On top is an engraved dedication: "In Loving Memory of Benji." I don't take my eyes off this once beautiful creature, perfectly frozen in time, looming over the front room. Goodness knows how much she must have paid to have the work done; the glass in the case is so thick, it would withstand an earthquake. Perhaps interviewing her will be worthwhile after all; I'm sure she can pick and choose any washing powder she likes.

The only photographs on the mantlepiece are of the dog, so I guess Benji to be her only kin. He isn't (wasn't) "just a dog," but the love of her life. As I sip my tea, I take out my forms to "interview" her, even if I will have to bin her responses the moment we are done. Then, when we're finished, I thank her profusely, say how beautiful Benji is and bid her goodbye.

For everyone else who answers my surveys, I take down their name, address and contact details. Head Office checks up randomly to monitor that we researchers are doing the job correctly and not cheating by filling in the surveys ourselves. I find it a slog to persuade members of the public to talk to me, especially as the questions are so mundane. Talking to consumers about their favourite brands of washing-up liquid or soap powder is vastly different from the research I did for a documentary on lifestyle where social groups answered questions about their voting behaviour and the state of the economy.

Six months later, at the end of a wet, cold and miserable day in Hulme, I don't have enough forms completed and I've reached the limit of my endurance. I pull out six forms and fill in the surveys, giving fictitious names for addresses in the street I last visited, then drive home, throw the fake surveys away and hand in my notice.

11

Carry On Doctor

Newcastle-upon-Tyne, 1990
I don't yet have a TV job; I have been interviewed three times for a corporate role at Mersey Television, but each time, I lose out. Because there are no other TV jobs going in Liverpool, I apply for a role as Production Manager in Newcastle-upon-Tyne with a startup making medical videos. If I'm successful, I will no longer be anyone's assistant and will finally get to call myself a manager. I will be responsible for budgeting, scheduling and staff, including a secretary and production assistant.

I am invited back for a second interview on 22 November to meet the bosses from the ITV regional franchise holder, Tyne Tees Television, and the medical school—this startup is planned to be a joint venture. As I sit in the reception, a news-flash on the TV shows a tearful Margaret Thatcher announcing her resignation as Prime Minister. This being the North East, which the Tories under Thatcher plunged into a hotbed of unemployment after closing down all the heavy industry and coalmines, a cheer goes up from staff who pour out of their offices to witness this historic moment.

A bad day for Margaret Thatcher is a successful one for me. I think the interview panel members may have already made their decision as this is more of a rubber-stamping exercise. I have plenty of time to think about the job on my three-hour drive home, so that evening, when one of the interviewers rings to offer me a well-paid permanent role, I accept on the spot. The security this represents when I was anticipating a fixed contract is too good a deal to turn down. It's only when I put the phone down, I remember the downside: back on the treadmill of weekly commuting.

I don't want to move into a house share, so I rent a small flat in Jesmond, a leafy middle-class neighbourhood close to my new office. A large Victorian house has been divided up into four flats, but mine is unfurnished, drab and unloved. On the plus side, it has its own cooking facilities and bathroom, and I will feel safe there at night.

I set about finding some basic furniture and a bed, but when I move in, I realise just how cold the flat is. The single-glazed sash windows are no match for the bitterly icy winds blowing off the North Sea. As I'll only be there four nights a week, I console myself with the fact my flat is near a park. I can at least go for a run before work.

Because the company is a startup, it is three months before we begin making any videos as there are scripts to write and filming to organise. My colleagues are easy-going, except the Production Assistant—who would have to be the person I line manage. It transpires she has a chip on her shoulder the size of the Tyne Bridge and is miffed that the company hired "a Southerner." The irony of being labelled a Southerner when I grew up in New Zealand isn't lost on me. I know I won't win her over, but her hostile act brings me down so much, I have to steel myself to go into the office each day.

I drive into work on Fridays so that I can go straight home to Liverpool from there. At 5pm sharp at the end of that first week, I breathe a sigh of relief. I even have my pound coin ready for the Mersey Tunnel so I can get home as quickly as possible.

It's mid-winter, so when the alarm goes off at 4.45 on Monday morning, it's so dark outside, it could be midnight. When I'm organised, I pack a bag the night before; if I forget, it's a mad scramble to be out the door at 5.30am. The trip takes three hours, but as the weather deteriorates, I allow myself some wriggle room.

The road is flat until I reach Lancaster; there, it climbs just before the University where I spent a semester teaching Documentary Production. Of all the academic jobs that I've done—hourly paid part-time Lecturer; Writing Tutor in adult education at various institutions—Lancaster was far and away the best. Not only was I paid as a freelancer and given a full day's work a week during the semester, I got a fancy job title—Associate Lecturer—and an office to myself. I would have stayed on if the academic who employed me hadn't resigned; I wonder where my career would have gone if they hadn't left.

Throughout the winter, I drive through sleet, snow, gales, but the worst is fog, when I can barely see the brake lights of the car in front. As long as I keep up with the traffic, I don't mind how long it takes me to get to the services at Shap, the highest point of the M6. But if I'm there by 7am, that gives me 30 minutes to refuel, grab breakfast, inhale some fresh air and get on my way again.

By 7.30am, the traffic is backing up. Once I turn off at Carlisle and head east towards Newcastle, I join the thousands of commuters who do this drive every day. One time, I swear I see a wallaby hopping along in a field beside Hadrian's Wall. Maybe I've been spending too much time alone. But as wallabies do actually exist, my sighting is far less fanciful than those of a mythical beastie bobbing up and down in a certain lake north of the border.

The office closes for Christmas on Friday 21 December and doesn't re-open again until Wednesday 2 January. Back in Liverpool for the festive season, I meet Emma, an Arts Administrator, at a Christmas party, who does the same weekly commute as me by train. She offers to share fuel costs and I jump at the chance. It's stressful driving all that way on my own and I'll be glad of the company, even though it will mean a detour into the centre of Liverpool to pick her up. There's so little traffic early in the morning when I leave, it will add no more than ten minutes to my journey.

The first day we drive to Newcastle together, Emma settles herself down in the passenger seat and promptly falls asleep. It seems rude to turn on the radio as I don't want to wake her up, but it's a little disconcerting. So much for having company.

Is the journey going to be silent for the next three hours?

I have already briefed her about breaking the journey at Shap and she was fine with that. Well, when she was awake, she was.

What do I do?

As I slow down, take the exit for Shap services and find a place to park, I'm hoping Emma will wake up, but she's out cold. I feel guilty leaving her in the car on a bitter January day with no heating so try to be as quick as I can, but when I return, she still hasn't stirred.

Maybe she's frozen to death? No, she's breathing.

I crank on the heating as we set off, this time to refuel.

Despite the din from the petrol pump, Sleeping Beauty doesn't stir.

Wish I could sleep like that.

Two and a half hours into our journey, on the outskirts of Newcastle at 8.30am, Emma wakes up.

'Are we there yet?' she says, yawning and stretching.

If it had been the same story on the way home on Friday, I would have mutinied and told her to find her own way in future, but by then, she is charm itself. Our ambivalence towards our jobs is something we have in common and the return journey to Liverpool flies by as we chat about life, politics, relationships and everything in between.

* * *

In February 1991, a surgeon at the medical school makes a request for my team to film a teaching video of a live demonstration of keyhole surgery. Watching will be medical students in the UK and beyond, so it's a big deal. I have full confidence in the film crew—all regulars, experienced in news, outside broadcasts and the studio. As this is our first shoot, I accompany the team to mark the occasion.

We mask and gown up and put on the shoe covers. Then four of us—Camera Operator, Sound Operator, Producer-Director and me—troop into theatre. With the medical team and the patient, it's quite a squash in there. It's boiling hot and smells of raw meat and antiseptic.

The camera rolls as the Surgeon, who clearly fancies himself as a performer, plays to the audience while he greets the assembled clinicians. The patient, a woman in her 50s, is already out cold, which is just as well because there's an audience of at least thirty people plus a film crew watching the removal of her kidney stones; we did take the precaution of asking her to sign the filming consent form before she was anaesthetised.

The operation begins and the laser-guided catheter reaches the first kidney stone after about five minutes. So far, so routine. But when the laser fires into what is supposed to be the kidney stone to dissolve it, there's the unmistakable smell of burning flesh followed by a vertical spurt of blood. It jets up into the air like a geyser at Yellowstone.

I'm dimly aware that the Camera Operator cuts the live feed and stops filming. Luckily someone had the good sense to place a chair in the corner and I grab hold of it, sliding onto the seat. I put my head between my knees, willing myself not to throw up or pass out while the crew grab their gear and get out of there.

I look over my shoulder at the Surgeon who, along with his crash team, is frantically trying to save the patient's life. Luckily, he succeeds in bringing her back from the dead.

* * *

In May 1991, we sell our first corporate video, but the gossip is that the startup is haemorrhaging money, mostly on salaries. The young MBA graduate who wrote the business plan abruptly resigns, leaving the rest of us to wonder about our future. And then, just before my birthday, we are all called into the Managing Director's office.

'I hate to do this to you, but we've had to come to a hard decision. And I want to be straight with you,' says the MD. 'The company isn't sustainable. It turns out that the financial projections were overly optimistic.'

So the rumours are true.

'We'll be closing the business this Friday and will give

each of you six months' pay as your redundancy package. I'm very sorry.'

Yes! Oh joy, joy, joy. Six months on full salary to stay at home. Can life get any better than this?

After the boss delivers his bombshell, he leaves my team of five to it.

'Right,' says one. 'Let's all go to the pub, shall we?' We nod in unison. It's 5pm and the working day has ended.

'I don't have to give the company car back until Friday,' says the only teetotaller among us. 'Let's make the most of it.' I don't know how he wangled a convertible out of the startup, but we're glad he did. He pulls back the roof and the five of us pile in. Dizzy with our newfound freedom and good fortune, we zoom around Newcastle-upon-Tyne. After a few drinks and dinner, the initially hostile Production Assistant is now my best buddy.

We stagger into the office the next day nursing hangovers—apart from our designated driver, of course. Gone are the suits, and in their place are jeans and t-shirts. I am due to renew the lease on my flat, but luckily have yet to sign any paperwork. The estate agent allows me fewer than two days to sell my furniture, move out, clean up and give the keys back.

After saying my goodbyes to my team, I leave for home at the usual time on Friday afternoon. As Emma gets in the car, we turn to each other and say the same thing at the same time.

'You'll never guess…'

'You go first,' Emma says.

'I've been made redundant,' I reply. She throws back her head and roars with laughter.

'Me too.'

We are still laughing when we get to Liverpool.

12

Christmas Cracker

Manchester, 1991

I stash my redundancy money away and accept a job as Production Manager with a community action magazine programme that goes out on Granada after the six o'clock news. The only drawback is that the production office is in Manchester, a three-hour round-trip by car from our home in The Wirral. Taking the train is rarely an option because of my irregular working hours.

Despite the long commute, I look forward to work every morning as the team are a friendly bunch. And because a sizeable amount of the programming we make is about social justice issues, there's a feel-good factor to the daily grind. I enjoy the environment and go about my work with enthusiasm. When at the Christmas party, the bosses inform us that another series has been commissioned, we cheer and drink a toast.

Then Jo, the Executive Producer, and her sidekick, Senior Producer Robert, say they have an announcement. Robert has a piece of paper in his hand.

'Do you want to tell them or shall I?' Jo says. I glance

around at my colleagues to see if any of them know what's going on. By their body language, it doesn't look like it, though I notice one sitting bolt upright. She glances away when I look at her.

'If I call your name, we'd like you back for the new series,' Robert says smugly. Does that mean some of us won't be back? What a time to tell us!

I knew there was a reason I've never liked him.

The previously jolly atmosphere falls flat. We put our glasses down and no one is game to break the silence. I glance at my colleague again. She's smirking.

She's in on it.

One of my teammates nudges me. 'Here we go,' she whispers.

'If I don't call your name, we won't be renewing your contract.'

Robert becomes Master of Ceremonies in a bizarre game of musical chairs. 'Luke, you're safe.' As the names are called one by one, there's clapping from the lucky group who are to keep their jobs, while the rest of us sit silently, waiting to know our fate.

And then there are three.

'Bastards,' the woman opposite me mutters. There's a yawning gap between the "winners" and the "losers" as Queen Bee Jo summons the chosen ones to the end of the table, while we rejected three pour the remaining wine and drown our sorrows. Once we've drunk our fill of the free booze and coffee, we bid our farewells, thanking the Producers for the party on the way out.

'Screw them,' one of my colleagues says. 'Come on, let's find a bar.'

'And we can plan what to do next,' says the other, the sensible one of the trio.

This is my first experience of being shafted at work, but it won't be my last. The irony isn't lost on me that this vindictive humiliation of the staff doesn't exactly reflect the community-spirited values of the series we've worked on. And I'm cross with myself for believing in the Producers. They sold me a sob story about the company not being able to afford commercial rates and I agreed to take less money because of it. To use the Christmas meal to get rid of staff is such a cheap shot. It's brutal.

I'm disillusioned, but this may just be the impetus I need to further my career. I'm going to upskill.

* * *

The Cotswolds, 1991
I persuade a writer friend to join me on a residential weekend course on writing for television. We set off for the Cotswolds and arrive at the Three Ways House Hotel in Mickleton, Gloucestershire. Its claim to fame is that it's home to the Pudding Club, created to preserve the tradition of the British pudding, so as soon as we're settled, we set off on a country walk in anticipation of a surfeit of delicious desserts. Instead, we're chased across a wheat field by a ferocious pit bull terrier.

We recover from our ordeal with the aid of a soothing gin and tonic, and then turn our attention to our fellow participants. What will they be like? We may not get on with them. But at least we'll have each other.

It doesn't take us long to get the measure of at least two of them. A septuagenarian couple are not only addicted to self-improvement, they don't miss an opportunity to talk about themselves to anyone they can ambush. They've only just finished a photography course, so in their opinion, they're doing us all a massive favour by coming on this one. The following weekend, they're due to go on one about travel writing. I can't keep up with them.

'I would like to write for the television,' the wife states as we all introduce ourselves to the other participants at the first session of the weekend, 'but I'd prefer not to have to write smut. There's so much sex on TV nowadays. Would I have to do that?' How the Course Convenor keeps a straight face, I don't know.

'Well,' he says, 'it's up to you what you put in your scripts. You don't have to put in any sex. And if you want to change the culture of TV drama, it's in your hands.'

'Oh well, in that case, it sounds like I'm perfect for the job,' she says.

The Convenor, it seems, is a seasoned pro at dealing with the participants who are rather too puffed up with their own self-importance. We don't hear any more from her in class for the rest of the weekend and make sure we sit well away from her at mealtimes.

One of our tutors is a series producer who worked on *Teachers*, the comedy drama I fielded complaints about a few years ago. Before the course, we were asked to submit the outline and five pages of a script for a TV drama in advance of a one-to-one with her. I know I'm going to like her; her feedback is so encouraging, I think of little else long after the weekend is over. It lifts my spirits and carries me through what is to be one of the most challenging years of my life.

* * *

By 1992, Mum's mental health has declined so much that my sister and I take turns to fly to New Zealand to care for her.

While I am looking after her, I apply for an MA in Scriptwriting at the Northern Film School in Leeds. The Course Leader wrote a highly praised screenwriting textbook, which helped me shape my application, but as it's one of only two such courses in the country, my chances of an interview are slim.

I try not to get my hopes up and turn my attention to looking after Mum. Her needs are complex and too hard to manage from the other side of the world, so my sister and I make the decision to bring her to the UK so that we can share her care. My sister travels back to New Zealand to accompany her on the long flight. But while we are frantically searching for a care home for her, she dies in tragic circumstances, falling from an intercity train after a week's visit with me.

We make the decision that Mum's funeral will be held back in New Zealand, and my sister and I travel from the UK. It's a traumatic and distressing time to say the least, but on the day I arrive home after Mum's funeral, there is a letter waiting for me from the film school, inviting me for interview. This lifts my spirits like nothing else, which is exactly what I need right now as I still have the circumstances surrounding Mum's death to deal with.

A lawyer contact puts me in touch with one of his colleagues, who is representing dozens of families who have lost relatives in similar incidents. When I go to see him in his tiny office above a shop in a run-down shopping centre, he agrees to take on our case for a very modest fee as he is building a class action court case against the state-owned rail operator British Rail.

When the case finally goes to court, it turns out that British Rail has kept quiet about hundreds of train deaths over the years, while the UK government has been too busy privatising the railways and selling them off to the highest bidder to take any notice. We are not out for financial gain, instead demanding safety improvements so that other families never have to go through what we had to. And against all the odds, this modest one-man band from the North West wins the case, despite having to face off some of the best and most highly paid government-appointed silks in the land.

On the train from Liverpool Lime Street to Leeds, a journey which in the middle of the day takes two hours, I go over my written application. The bulk of it is a screenplay for a short film. If it's selected by a student director at the film school, I will be guaranteed to have it produced; it was for this reason alone that I applied. An MA might be useful if I want to pick up some hourly paid teaching at a university, but will make no difference to my production career. The standard industry calling card is a short film, particularly one that wins awards at film festivals.

When I arrive at the interview, I'm astonished to find that the Course Leader has moved on and her replacement is now in charge of recruiting. Luckily, we hit it off. I spend the trip back gazing out of the window, thinking about Mum. She was the one who gave me a love of reading, writing and the theatre. As the train rumbles along on the rickety track and the industrial landscape turns to moorland, I can think of no more fitting use for the money I will be inheriting than pursuing a career where I can combine production with scriptwriting. I just hope my interview has been successful.

I don't have to wait long. On the Friday, I get another letter from the Northern Film School, offering me a place.

* * *

Leeds, 1994

Twenty-four of us on the screenwriting course compete for twelve slots that will see our screenplays made into films. We are quietly competitive—we all want this badly and have made sacrifices to be here. When we pitch our scripts to the Directors, the dynamic between us changes.

The odds are even. Then two writers drop out, increasing the chances for the rest of us. In this industry, the stakes are high and there are no guarantees, just as there aren't in life. I push my negative thoughts aside, but it's hard not to fret.

And then I receive a call from one of the best directors on the course. He loves my screenplay, but is worried an unconventional story with two older protagonists might not be commercial enough as his calling card. He wants to work in TV drama rather than film. I am both buoyed and anxious.

What if the other directors think that too?

Then a Polish Director, Maciej, who is on the course through the Erasmus European exchange programme gets in touch. He's excited by the technical possibilities my script presents, but wants to focus on the darker aspects of the story. This isn't exactly what I envisaged, but that's the only change he intends to make, so I say yes.

Our next task is to approach a producer on the Production Course. The Producer Maciej and I both want says yes, but she can't be hands on as she's got her schedule full with another film. I offer to step in and line produce if her team will act as Executive Producers. It's a win-win for both sides as the official Producer gets the credit, even though I do the lion's share of the work, which doesn't bother me as I'm working in the industry I want to be in. As well as problem-solving how to get my film made, I am deliberately keeping busy with creative work while I have the ordeal of Mum's inquest hanging over me.

I based my screenplay, called *Christmas Cracker*, on a story from my childhood about a family Christmas that goes horribly wrong. The main characters are in their 70s as one of the themes deals with ageing, a subject that commercial cinema rarely addresses. As it's a studio-based film, a large chunk of the budget is eaten up by set design as one of the characters is obsessed with his model train set.

I've costed enough productions to know that the budget allocated by the film school won't be enough. And with barely three months before we start principal photography, I badly need sponsors, and beg and borrow as much as I can. My Producer is a close relative of the co-star of the hit sitcom *Keeping Up Appearances*, who graciously agrees to come on board. Once we confirm that she is to star, the sponsorship rolls in.

In my role as Line Producer, I turn a friend's house in Liverpool into a film set and accommodation for the crew. A local catering college does all the catering for our five shoot days, cooking lunch and providing us with tea, coffee, cakes and biscuits. These are long filming days and the least we can do to keep our volunteer crew happy is to feed them properly.

I'm so grateful for the donations, community support and goodwill that enable us to make this film. But it's when I don my other "hat" as a writer that I get so much more out of the experience. In rehearsal, I hear for the first time professional actors saying aloud the words I've written. Suddenly my story has come to life. And when the leading actress suggests a couple of small but significant line changes in her dialogue, it feels like a true collaboration.

By early summer, we've finished editing, but once post-production is over, I have no money left for marketing—when I budgeted for film school, I didn't include the cost of distributing my graduation film. By then, it's just me applying for screenings; I'm selective and only choose the higher-profile ones that give out awards, paying to send physical copies of VHS tapes by post to international film festivals.

Christmas Cracker is screened at Leeds International Film Festival, where it is well received, and in Spain at the L'Alternativa Independent Film Festival in Barcelona. Even though I'm desperate to go, I'm unable to attend the festival screening in Spain as I don't have the money, nor can I spare the time.

I've been so busy with the film, I have yet to complete the theory part of my master's degree: the 10,000 word dissertation. Without that, I won't be able to graduate. While I try to finish that, I feel the pressure to earn again to make up for the loss of income. It can't be any old job, either; it has to be well paid.

I cast my net wide. London has the lion's share of production jobs, but I'm forced to factor in the weekly commuting, plus the cost of accommodation. But the Big Smoke is calling me back, and it's not long before I take heed.

13

London Calling

At my second interview for the job of Production Manager on *The Big Breakfast*—Channel 4's madcap, anarchic morning programme—the interviewer, John, scans my CV for a production company he recognises. He's going to struggle. I've done my homework and found out his background is in sport and outside broadcasts, so we'll have difficulty finding common ground. The nearest I've got to a recognisable brand is the community action programme for Granada, but that was the north of England so probably doesn't count.

His eyes fall upon a job I did two years ago, which I haven't even given a second thought as it wasn't for broadcast. I produced a testimonial video for Heart of Midlothian, a Scottish Premier League football club.

'What did you enjoy most about working on this project?' he asks.

'Seeing inside the gin palaces of minor Scottish football celebrities and checking out their light fittings.'

That seems to break the ice. He then confides that I'm

the twelfth interviewee on the short list, and so far, the others have all failed his killer question.

How will I know the answer when they didn't?

I have a debt from film school and have had no real income for eighteen months, so there's a lot riding on this.

'What would you do if the satellite link went down during a live broadcast?' He rocks back in his chair. 'Take your time.' He may have the killer question, but I already know the killer answer. He's forgotten that at the first interview, he boasted about this "gotcha" question and we discussed it at some length. Rather than rushing in with an answer, I pretend to concentrate. I see the reflection of my expression in his glass office walls; it looks alarming.

'Get on the roof and repoint the dish?' 'You're nearly there,' he encourages.

If I play it right, this one's in the bag, but I don't want to answer too quickly.

'Get a runner to do it?'

'Yeah, and the posher, the better. One whose father earns more than the GDP of Malaysia.' John is a plain-looking working-class lad from Essex and I'm from the Antipodes without money, influence, or connections, so he clearly thinks we're kindred spirits.

Time to go in for the kill. 'The only thing you can do is switch back to the studio and hope the engineers fix the problem, or continue the item with sound only via a mobile phone.'

He looks startled, but pleased. 'Right, you're in,' he announces.

I've done it. I know diddly squat about outside broadcasts or satellite links and have only ever worked on two live events, but out of all the candidates, he's chosen me because I'm an outsider. Just like him.

I sense a presence behind me as John practically prostrates himself on the carpet. The MD, it seems, is here. He asks me to stand up, then rather like a farmer checking out the cattle at the sales yard before he bids for them, he walks around me. 'As long as you're not a dragon, you'll be alright,' he says.

I may not be a dragon, but I do seem to be years older than most at the company. Even the MD hasn't reached his thirtieth birthday. But I walk out as though I've won the pools. Well, in a way, I have.

I wait for the train to Bank at South Quay station in Docklands, a futuristic city that looks like it's made of Lego, to make my way to Euston. By the time I arrive back at Lime Street, it's dark, and the stairwell and lifts to the carpark are closed. We commuters have no choice but to risk life and limb and walk into the oncoming traffic hurtling down the ramp. On the drive home through the Wallasey Tunnel, I work out how long it'll take me to pay off my debts. Five hundred and fifty pounds a week seems like a hell of a lot of money to me, but I realise too late that I should have negotiated. I bet the Production Manager on *The Word* is paid more than me. And as I'll once again be spending my weeks in London, my wages will soon go.

* * *

A week later, I'm back at Lime Street station at the inhumane hour of 5.45am, ready to make the trek to Euston. I'm grateful that it's summer and daylight. As the train curves its way over the Runcorn Bridge, I look longingly across the estuary towards home.

Putting thoughts of homesickness aside, I close my eyes as we pass Crewe Station and count down the seconds until three minutes have passed. When I took the job, I knew I'd have to pass the spot where Mum died after falling from that train with the defective doors. As we pick up speed, a fox, hidden in a field of wheat, pops its head up and stares straight at me. It lifts my spirits to encounter a wild animal in its prime, going about its daily life. It's time for me to do the same.

At seven, I go to the snack bar and buy myself a milky boiled coffee, which is bitter and scalding hot in its Polystyrene cup. Even with the lid off, I'm too scared to drink it in case the train lurches across the points and I burn the inside of my mouth. By the time we reach Stafford, the coffee has cooled. As I dip a flabby factory-made croissant into it, I realise this is likely to be my Monday morning breakfast for the next year.

At Watford, I'm getting cold feet about taking this job.
Can I do this?

As the train slows down to head into Euston, we pass the building where I'd once worked as Location Manager for a National Film School student who has since become a successful Hollywood Director. Like most people who work on freebies, I always kid myself that this guy or gal will be the next big thing. Well, he certainly was, roaring off to Tinseltown faster than it took to snort a line of coke, conveniently forgetting the team who helped get him there. I thought a BAFTA award-winner on my CV would open doors, but that film has never even landed me an interview.

At Euston, I navigate my way through the Underground, not by the names of the stations, but by the colour on the Tube map. It's light blue east until the red, black and DLR intersect.

It's 8.30am and I've been told to come in for 10am. I don't want to be too early, but I need to offload my suitcase and backpack. My shoulders ache so I decide to go straight to the office. By the time a DLR train turns up with enough room for me to squeeze on to it, it's already gone 9am.

I haul my bags out of the station at South Quay. Surely there is somewhere that sells coffee, even in the no-man's-land that is Docklands. At Canary Wharf, where all the banks are, it would be easy to find a cafe, but South Quay has one lone sandwich bar. At least there is somewhere to sit.

After I've had my caffeine hit, I make my way to the office, dragging my case behind me. I meet the Head of Human Resources. After showing me where I can park my stuff, she begins the induction process. She escorts me around to meet the various heads of department, and then I sit down at my desk as the Sandwich Man arrives. My team of two Coordinators are just about to run through what they do, but break off to ask me if I want to join the line for food. The lunch choices are him or the sandwich bar where I bought my coffee, so naturally, I choose him. Not even Hollywood royalty is as popular as the Sandwich Man.

The Friday of my first week coincides with the monthly champagne breakfast at Big Breakfast House, where the programmes are filmed. This is mostly a PR exercises for the benefit of the press and the executives who fund the programme. As the studio in Old Ford Lock is a conversion from three terraced houses, the gardens have been merged into one impressive lawn stretching for half an acre. It's easily big enough for a marquee. There's a string quartet in formal dress at one end, and the great and the good at the other.

By 9.30am, I'm working the room, holding a glass of champagne. I'm introduced to an array of television people whose faces I should recognise, but I forget who they are in an instant. The people I need to get onside are the heads of the departments I'm in charge of—Camera, Sound, Vision Mixing, Lighting, Set Design, Hair and Make-up. There are so many staff, I don't see how I will manage to run the studio when I'm not based onsite. Fortunately, I have a rock-solid Site Manager; from our first meeting, she has come across as matter of fact and helpful, so I can tell she will be my eyes and ears on set at the times I can't be there. As the call time for the presenters and crew is 3.45am, ready for rehearsals and the live show from 7–9am, that will be nearly all the time. By 9.45am, I'm anxious to get to my desk, so I grab a lift from a colleague. The distance between the two sites is just over four miles by road. Fortunately, the traffic isn't too bad and I'm at my workstation at 10. Even though I was up just after 5 and got to work for 7, my day is only really beginning now. It's just as well I stuck to one glass of bubbly.

I plan my Friday afternoon escape with precision. To make the Liverpool train on time, I have to be out of the office by 6pm and at the Docklands Light Railway platform for 6.10pm. With far fewer scheduled trains than the London Underground going at a snail's pace, the DLR takes ten minutes to reach Bank Station.

The Northern Line interchange at Bank takes ages to reach as the station is deep underground and the escalator seems to go on forever. And I'm carrying luggage so I'm not able to walk down it. I've allowed five minutes for the interchange, which takes ten, and by now it's 6.30pm. It's five years since I last worked in London and I've forgotten the hell of Fridays at rush hour on the Underground.

I emerge from the bowels of the earth at King's Cross and walk the rest of the way along Euston Road, inhaling the traffic fumes of what must be one of the most polluted roads in Europe. By now, it's 6.50pm and my train departs at

7.10. And the line for the train is already snaking around the corner. I've bought a return ticket, saving myself precious minutes which I use to stock up with junk magazines at the WH Smith concession in the station.

While everyone else runs clutching a drink and a sandwich, I stroll nonchalantly along as I plan to spend the journey in the dining car. Second-class ticket holders are allowed in the first-class dining carriage, providing we buy dinner. That costs over twenty pounds, which is quite steep.

I am the only woman in the carriage. My fellow passengers are a mix of City types and, judging by the amount of paperwork they have with them, lawyers who have spent their week in the High Court. Given that I am probably the only one who can't claim their meal on expenses, dinner on the train is a real treat. Even Watford doesn't look so bad as I pass it, gin and tonic in hand.

I can't manage three courses, but have a starter, a main and a coffee, which comes with a couple of mints. Once we second-class passengers finish our meals, we are meant to return to our allocated seats. But I love the dining car and spin the meal out, making myself so comfortable that by the time I finish, the staff clearly don't have the heart to ask me to move.

The train gets into Lime Street just after 10pm, so that means a Friday-night social life in Liverpool is out of the question. But who needs a social life when waiting to pick me up is my beloved?

14

I'm a Celebrity

A Researcher and a Producer take turns coming up with a week's worth of *Big Breakfast* content—ten hours of live television—finding their crazy, offbeat stories mainly through magazines and newspapers, which are kept in the Information Centre on the second floor. Once they choose their item, they then have to find the phone numbers of the people they want to invite to be on the show. The only way of doing that is to look through printed telephone directories like the *Yellow Pages*, or if nothing is listed there, call 192 Directory Enquiries, charged at 40p a minute. When management gets the phone bill and sees that everyone in the office has been bypassing the printed directories and dialling this premium phone line, they put an immediate stop to our unrestricted telephone access.

In 1995, I opt to take on an additional production called *The Weekend Show*, a weekly magazine programme presented by Dale Winton and Liza Tarbuck, which opens up an opportunity to employ more researchers. While we are interviewing researchers for the job, after sifting through hundreds of CVs, I sit down with the Producer to come up with our "gotcha" questions: 'Who is the Chancellor of the Exchequer?' and 'How do you find a Druid?'

Out of the eight candidates who make the shortlist, only half answer both correctly. They've clearly read a newspaper recently and know about ancient Celtic cultures. One poor unfortunate guesses Ken Clarke correctly, but doesn't seem to know what a Druid is; he suggests the *Yellow Pages* as a likely place to start. We play along and invite him to show us precisely where in the *Yellow Pages* he'd find one, hoping that once he realises that no such listing exists, he'll suggest places in England where Druids hang out. Sadly, neither Stonehenge nor Glastonbury are on his radar. It might sound like a mean process, but if a budding researcher can't answer a gotcha question, they'll never be able to cope with the demands of breakfast television.

For the Researcher and Producer running the Monday-to-Friday *Big Breakfast* show, work starts on the Sunday. They work through the night to get their scripts written, approved, typed, then timed by the Script Supervisor ready for photocopying by 2am. At 3.45am, they have to be at Big Breakfast House for the first script meeting with the Director, followed by the Presenters, then the Floor team. The show goes on-air at 7am, and even though it has all been planned on paper, there are constant last-minute changes to the running order. Items get dropped, moved around and added at such a frenetic pace, it's exhausting even to write about it.

Once Monday's show is off air, there's no let up as the team has to prepare for the next day's show, often not leaving the office until past midnight. Then, if they're lucky, they might catch a couple of hours' sleep before their 3.45am call time down at the studio.

Given that the Production teams must work through the

night one week in three, nearly all the staff are young and childless. There is just one Producer with a family who does overnights, and the only jobs going for women with dependents are the weekly inserts like Zig and Zig. A family-friendly work culture doesn't exist in television, and it's always the women with families whose careers suffer. By 40, most of them have left the industry. In film production the attrition rate is higher still, especially as the job often involves filming abroad.

When Production has booked the guests, my team of Coordinators organise accommodation for the night before, if they don't live in London, and transport to the set. Depending on the item, each show can involve twenty to thirty guests. Because they have to fill two hours of screen time, the teams tend to neglect the non-celebrity guests, knowing that they'll need to drop at least some of them at short notice. These guests sit around forlornly in a draughty Portakabin waiting to go on, but if the team axes their segment, the only compensation is a free hot breakfast with the cast and crew after the show, along with all their expenses paid. And it doesn't matter if they dropped everything to travel to be on the show—that's it.

Understandably, this causes friction with some guests who, having agreed to take part in a TV show, end up only getting a fry-up. If they're really aggrieved and/or media-savvy, they call up a tabloid journalist to complain, but unless they have a newsworthy story, such as having to leave a sick child with minders or quitting their job to be on the programme, they often don't get very far. Today I guess they would vent their anger on social media.

As it is my job to help make all the madcap things the Producers dream up happen, I am the grown-up saying yes, you can do such-and-such, but with conditions attached.

My biggest fear is that under my watch, a presenter or a member of the public will either be seriously injured or die. And if that sounds overly dramatic, bear in mind that I was the person who gave permission for Presenter Keith Chegwin to be strapped on to the front of a 1940s bi-plane and go wing walking for his last appearance on the segment *Down Your Doorstep*. If you search on YouTube for "Keith Chegwin Wing Walking (*Big Breakfast* 95)," you'll see that Keith is miked up so that we can not only see him, we can hear him as he takes us through every terrifying second of this stunt.

Of all the Presenters, Keith, along with Mark Little, is my favourite. Keith is so cheerful and uncomplaining, and whenever he comes into the office, he always drops by to say hello. When a floor manager—who works for our competition, but wants to do more work with us—casually lets slip that TVAM is sending a crew to cover the British cricket team on their South African tour, I alert the Executive Producers. But they don't confirm until Friday afternoon that we will be doing an outside broadcast from South Africa and Zimbabwe, following the England cricket team ourselves.

Cricket isn't normal fodder for *Down Your Doorstep*, so the Production team has to find a different angle. Can they film the England squad practising yoga, at a game park, or supporting charities? And can Keith interview Archbishop Desmond Tutu?

It's my job to organise all the live satellite links—as South Africa is in the same time zone as the UK, we are planning to do most of the broadcasts live. This will hopefully work in the major African cities, but in the more remote areas in Zimbabwe, it's doubtful we'll find a signal.

To be on the safe side, these inserts will be pre-recorded and sent down the line for the following day's show.

It's one thing to set up an outside broadcast in the UK with companies I know and trust, it's quite another to have to do so on a different continent. There are outside broadcast companies who do regular work for international news crews in South Africa, but Zimbabwe proves to be much more challenging. Anyone who is any good has been booked up for months; as usual, we've left it to the last minute.

As the world's media is about to descend upon South Africa, I beg and plead until I find a company at the eleventh hour prepared to help us. Then I go over all the sound and camera equipment we need for the broadcast for the umpteenth time and send the final list over to South Africa. After booking all the satellite links and praying that the co-ordinates we've provided are accurate, all I can do is wait and worry.

With the technical part of the trip locked in, the next hurdle is to find Keith and his Assistant Producer a flight. Keith, who is up for anything and relishing his career comeback, drops by after the *Down Your Doorstep* team meeting. A reformed alcoholic, he hasn't been able to kick his smoking habit and tells me he doesn't think he'll be able to cope with a twelve-hour flight without a cigarette. But British Airways has banned smoking and it's becoming increasingly difficult to find an airline that will allow it. Fortunately, South African Airways is one of the few left that does, and we find two of the last remaining seats to Cape Town.

After the first day's outside broadcast in Africa, which has come from a fairly large town, it's an enormous relief that it has all gone smoothly. The following day is a pre-record, so I sleep that night. I'm most worried about a remote area out in the bush. The common problem we have isn't losing picture, but sound. Our outside broadcast team uses a mobile phone when the link fails, but this is a last resort as the sound on the Presenter's piece to camera lags behind the picture.

In the weekly post-mortem after Friday's programme, I'll be the one who gets yelled at about this, even though I'm thousands of miles away from the location. One boss has a wildly unpredictable temperament, and when he's in a foul mood, I keep out of his way. But the viewer feedback from the South African tour has been so good that he comes into the meeting beaming from ear to ear. Far from bawling me out, he praises me, telling me that when the comms failed and Keith used his mobile phone, it proved to the viewers that the broadcast was indeed live.

I return to my work station, too stunned to speak. 'What's wrong?' a friend asks, her face full of concern.

'Bad Cop only went and said he didn't mind that the sound on the outside broadcast went down.'

'What's wrong with him?' I shrug, and then grin.

'The Prozac must be working.'

* * *

The good vibes continue right through to the end of the cricket tour as the *Down Your Doorstep* crew does manage to score an interview with none other than the Archbishop of Cape Town, Desmond Tutu. In a moment of pure comedy gold, Keith Chegwin gently enquires whether the great man has ever, in fact, worn a tutu. There is silence. Has the Archbishop misheard the question? Then a look of sheer delight crosses his face and he throws his head back and roars with laughter.

'Nobody has ever asked me that before,' he splutters, taking off his glasses and wiping his eyes, trying but failing to compose himself.

Unlike our rivals, we don't do sad stories or show confrontational news. Our target audience is 16–35-year-olds and the young at heart. If someone asks me what I achieve working on this programme, it's that I cheer viewers up and help make a lot of children late for school. It might be a little too late now to apologise to their parents.

Planet 24 produces *The Big Breakfast* and the equally anarchic Friday evening show *The Word*. Planet also runs an additional department, the Development Team, huddled away in another part of the second floor, pitching programme formats for future franchise productions. Development is a revolving door, with teams on short-term contracts. I recognise some faces, but it's hard enough keeping up with the freelancers who work at Big Breakfast House, let alone the new Development staff. It seems like every week, it's someone's birthday. And muggins here often ends up collecting money for presents and various causes.

I come to the desk of one of my favourite Assistant Producers. Normally, he's up for a laugh, but today, he's adopting such a defensive pose, he almost turns his back on me.

What's got into him?

I cut him some slack. He's been working through the night all week, which is enough to turn the mildest mannered person into a sleep-deprived monster, ready to lash out at the nearest victim.

'I'm collecting for Rwanda.' I jiggle the money box. He swings his chair around and gives me the evils.

'I don't effing know who she is, so why should I have to cough up for her birthday present?'

A staccato burst of laughter ricochets around the office. 'What,' he says, 'is up with you lot? I've had no bloody sleep for three days.'

I give him the side-eye. 'Are you for real?' *This is like a sketch in The Fast Show.* 'Err Rwanda isn't a person, it's a place.' I say.

Before I can say anything else, a booming voice from the other side of the office shouts, 'It's in war-torn Africa, mate. You know, where celebs raise money?'

'Oh shit. That Rwanda,' the Assistant Producer says, looking sheepish and casting frantically around for his wallet.

* * *

The Celebrity Booker has a contacts list that she practically chains to her person, so jealously does she guard it. She knows every celebrity PR in town.

The most highly prized celebrity guest is old-school Hollywood glamour. These fading stars only roll into town when they need the money, and the latest (let's just call her Zou- Zou) is in London plugging her (ghost-written) memoirs. She agrees to appear on *The Big Breakfast* on one condition: that we pay the outrageous fee she demands in cash. As the only cash we dish out is in expenses, we have to concoct an expenses claim and cobble together enough receipts while Zou-Zou is in London.

Given her expensive tastes, that isn't difficult. She takes taxis everywhere and makes the driver wait outside while she shops at Harrods, eats lunch at Claridge's and buys her "groceries" (consisting mainly of caviar and Pol Roger champagne) at Fortnum & Mason. Zou-Zou acknowledges she likes to indulge herself when travelling. At home, she's very frugal, she claims.

You could have fooled me.

She tells the same tale to every chat-show host: frugality was a habit she learned from her eastern European parents, who had to flee their homeland when the Nazis invaded, eventually settling in the United States. She now tops up her income by collecting rich husbands. This shrewd wit, along with Zou-Zou's heavily accented English, makes her a natural for screwball comedy.

I arrange with the office to get the cash (Zou-Zou says it has to be in fresh bank notes, not dirty used ones), but I don't fancy going down to the Big Breakfast House alone with such a large amount of money. Instead, I go to the studio to oversee the paperwork as I won't hand over this much cash without a signed receipt. Then I have no choice: the money needs to be delivered.

Zou-Zou arrives in a specially hired limo and engages in brinkmanship. As she gets out, she spots the welcoming committee—me—waiting beside the bridge across the canal, which guests and crew alike are required to cross to reach the set.

'Hello, darlink,' she calls. 'Do you have my money?'

There's no sign of the screwball comedian now. 'I'm not setting foot on that bridge until you give it to me.'

What does she think I'll do? Run off with it?

Odd as it may seem to someone like Zou-Zou, I can't hand over cash to anyone appearing on the show without them signing a receipt and a release form, as that allows *The Big Breakfast* the right to broadcast the footage of them. But once she has the envelope, she seems reluctant to sign anything and is rather more interested in ensuring we haven't short- changed her.

When I get back to the office and look at the scrawl on the release form and the receipt, it doesn't seem to resemble Zou- Zou's signature in any way, shape or form. Fortunately for me, all Accounts care about is that they have receipts. And any old signature. I could have signed them myself.

15

God Save The Queen

Each week on the show, the acts become more outlandish and the producers vie with each other to see who can come up with the most death-defying stunts. We assign one of the team to produce the red-hot out-takes, which are packaged into a hilarious programme that we watch at the annual Christmas party. We produce a second set of out-takes—a cleaned-up version—as a clips show to be screened on Channel 4 on Christmas Day, so that all of us can take Christmas off.

What could possibly go wrong?

I don't know whether the on-air team at the broadcaster has simply got complacent or is short-staffed. Either way, nobody in transmission bothers to check the pre-recorded tape until Christmas morning. Can you guess what happens next? Yes, the red-hot tape has accidentally been sent over to be broadcast across the nation and is minutes away from going out on-air. Of course it doesn't help that down at the edit suite at Big Breakfast House, the wrong label was put on the tape. It's only thanks to a minor miracle—a motorbike courier being able to make his way rapidly across town on empty Christmas Day roads—that we get the right one to the broadcaster in time.

I am in a remote national park on holiday in Kenya when I get the call from my boss, telling me what's happened. Luckily, he thinks the mix-up is hilarious and congratulates me for a job well done.

That's just one of the many things that can go wrong in this job. Because *The Big Breakfast* is live on-air for two hours, five days a week, we have to be prepared to be interrupted and taken off-air in the case of an event of national importance occurring. Known as obit rehearsals, our preparation for these occasions come straight after the programme finishes at 9am. There's a protocol we follow and there are two scenarios we have to consider: either the Presenters are live on-air when the announcement has to be made, or Zig and Zag, the irreverent Irish puppets we use as inserts, are doing their thing. When we don't have Zig and Zag in, we have to improvise a handover in the middle of their insert. Then we all fall about laughing at how wrong it could go, especially if the puppets are in the middle of singing a parody song.

Either way, the Presenter has to say a few words, then hand over to our newsreader, who will by then be wearing a black tie and a sombre-looking jacket in order to guide the viewers over to Channel 4 News. All newsreaders have an obit outfit, ready to put on at short notice, but few of them will be throwing their dark jacket and tie on over a technicolour shirt like ours.

As usual in our team, no one takes the obit rehearsals seriously. On one particular occasion, the two Presenters are still fooling about when the Floor Manager of the day stops the crew on set clearing up. We're going in for an obit rehearsal.

'Quiet, please,' the Floor Manager bellows into an open mic so that the entire studio floor and beyond can hear.

From the gallery, the countdown begins. 'Ten, nine, eight...' At the count of three, the open mic is switched off and the Presenters carry on with their studio chat. Then the Floor Manager cues one of the Presenters, who cuts his banter with his co-host.

'That's all we've got time for, as we go to the break,' he says. But the next shot is of the Newsreader in his dark tie and a jacket that doesn't seem to fit properly. He's sitting at a desk, which is really the make-up table, trying to look solemn. It doesn't help that from the back of the studio, two electrical crew members, known as cable bashers, laugh just as he launches into his serious voice.

'We are interrupting this programme for an important announcement,' he intones. 'I will now hand you over to Channel 4 News.'

'Keep rolling,' comes a voice from the gallery. The cable bashers are still fooling around.

'News just in from Buckingham Palace,' the Newsreader continues. 'Her Majesty the Queen was taken ill at her royal residence in Sandringham last night. And in the early hours of this morning...'

'Cut,' shouts the Floor Manager, his microphone projecting his voice right across the complex and into the make-up and props rooms where various staff members are milling around, packing up for the day. Even the guests moving in and out of the canteen and around the garden can hear.

I have come down to Big Breakfast House that morning, hoping to see how a trainee floor assistant is settling in, but it appears she left before the rehearsal finished. I'd told her I'd see her in the canteen, but either she has forgotten or something else has come up. I'll just put it down to a misunderstanding, rationalising that I'll see her another day that week, and leave it at that. But as usual, things aren't going to turn out to be that simple.

As I'm walking out of the office that evening after an exhausting day, the Executive Producer calls out to me.

'Alison,' he says, his voice censorious.

Sounds ominous. What have I done now?

'I've got a tabloid journalist on the phone. They're threatening to run a story that there's been a cover up and a senior member of the Royal Family is dead. And he says that the story came from us.'

'What? As far as I know, all the Royals are in full health. We had an obit rehearsal today. But that was all...'

Then I have a nasty feeling I know what may have happened. I feel sick. The Executive Producer smiles sweetly, which makes me feel even worse.

'Don't worry, I've fobbed him off. But can you go down to the studio tomorrow first thing and find out who it was that leaked that story? And when you do, get rid of them, will you? Thanks. Have a nice evening.'

Have a nice evening?

After a sleepless night, I duly obey orders. I speak to all the heads of departments, but draw a blank until I get to the Props Team. One of them saw the Trainee Floor Assistant standing just outside the make-up room during the obit take. When the Floor Manager yelled, 'Cut', he then walked up to the gallery to check on the footage, playing the sequence to the entire building. Although he announced it was an obit rehearsal, as it was her first day on the job, the Trainee can't have understood what that is. Instead of joining the crew in the canteen for breakfast, she quietly slipped away to spread the word that Her Majesty had sadly passed away. And now, I'm the one who has to interrogate her.

Naturally, she denies being the source. She says that she doesn't even know any journalists; the only people she's told are her mum and her nana.

I can imagine the conversation: 'Mum, guess what? We'd just finished recording the show, and then the news came on. The Queen—she's died!'

'Nana, listen to this, will you? I've got some bad news. But at least you'll have something to talk about down at the bingo today.' To satisfy my bosses, I do the part of my job I hate the most and fire her. I feel like an ogre to be dashing this girl's hopes of working in TV. I know how that feels.

16

La La Land

One year at *The Big Breakfast* is the equivalent of one dog year. Okay I'm exaggerating. Perhaps five in the "real world." This is partly my fault as I opted for a contract which pays me more, but gives me no holidays, apart from Christmas week; I chose this option to cover my rent in London and a mortgage in Liverpool. But I'm burnt out and have had enough. I've learned all I can about live television and I'll be treading water if I stay. When Human Resources refuses to alter my contract, I hand in my notice.

I have no other job to go to, but I put feelers out and monitor *Broadcast* magazine and Monday's *Guardian* newspaper for media jobs. One, working as a producer for Buena Vista Productions, the TV division of Disney, asks for both production management and creative experience. I submit an application, including a VHS tape of my short film *Christmas Cracker*, and then make the most of my last few weeks working on *The Big Breakfast*.

Coincidentally, Disney gets in touch around the same time to see if *The Big Breakfast* will cover the 50th anniversary of Disneyland in California. The bosses agree, providing we can find a week's worth of stories to cover in Los Angeles, and assign a team for the week on location consisting of an assistant producer and a presenter. But it will be a struggle to co-ordinate the filming across five days. As I am due to leave the week after, I offer to help on location and the Executive Producer assigned to that week agrees.

I have an agenda, which I keep to myself. If by some miracle, Buena Vista Productions calls me in for an interview, having filmed at Disneyland is likely to give me an advantage over the other candidates. But first, I have to get permission from HR to go.

'I'll still be available on the end of a phone if there are any problems on *The Big Breakfast* that week,' I tell the HR team. 'But as most of the inserts are coming from LA anyway, I don't expect there will be many problems.'

The next day, Anne, the Head of HR, says yes.

This is going well.

Not only can I do some primary research on Disney, this will be my one and only chance to go on location before I leave. Perks in this job are few.

Then, three days before we're due to leave, Anne hauls me into her office.

'What's this I hear about you going to LA?' she demands.

'I asked you last week. You said it was fine. What's made you change your mind?'

She won't answer, instead turning her back on me. I persist.

'I've set everything up for the show while I'm away, as we agreed. And I've told the team I'm on the other end of a phone whenever they need me.'

She paces up and down her office in her black suit, looking for all the world like an angry crow.

'How dare you go behind my back like that?'

Talk about shifting the goalposts.

'We've been planning this for days. And it's a bit late to change your mind now. All the flights and the hotel are booked and paid for.' Then realisation dawns.

She's jealous, thinks we're going on one big jolly and that location filming isn't actual work.

'I'll show you the schedule. We leave on Monday afternoon, and ten hours later get in late afternoon LA time. Then the next morning, it's meeting the crew and straight on the road. And we don't come up for air until the long flight home on Friday.'

Anne says nothing and purses her lips. As she sucks on her imaginary lemon, I feel betrayed. But it's too late to do anything about it now. I have work to do, and I'm damned if I'm going to let her rain on my Disney parade.

On the day we fly out, Richard, the Presenter who's coming with us, is filming live for *Down Your Doorstep* in Devon, and the only way to get him to the airport in time for our flight to LA is to stick him on the back of a taxi bike for a hair-raising three-hour ride. As he takes off his bike helmet and pulls off his goggles, dead flies drop out of them.

He wipes his eyes while I usher him towards the check-in and plead with the woman on the desk to give him an upgrade. She takes one look at his bedraggled appearance and says no. Poor Richard is stuck in economy with me and the Assistant Producer, Alex, for ten hours. Oh, the glamour of working in television...

* * *

We base ourselves in Santa Monica at the DoubleTree Suites on Fourth Street, which is about as central a location as we can find, given that our schedule includes Disneyland at Anaheim, the *Saved By the Bell* set at Universal City, our hotel lounge area for celebrity interviews, Dudley Moore in Malibu, the Viper Room in Hollywood and West Hollywood for an interview with Jackie Collins. Because of the eight-hour time difference between LA and the UK, it will be the middle of the night here when the show is on air at 7am in London, so everything we do has to be pre-recorded.

The plan is to bring all the tapes apart from the *Friends* interviews back with us to be edited. I've gone to some effort to hire the video equipment we use in the UK as opposed to the American standard, so that the footage we bring back won't need transferring. For once, I'm being proactive. I pat myself on the back.

On Tuesday morning, after a decent night's sleep, I wake early and throw on my gym gear. We're due to meet the crew at nine, so after a workout and shower, I wander down to breakfast, where I bump into Alex and Richard. The first location is the Viper Room, where Richard is filming a tribute to the young actor River Phoenix who died there. What I don't know is that LA's rush hour lasts until 10am, so our trip down the I-10 is a stop-start process, and what should have taken twenty minutes takes forty. But we have left early enough that we have time for a quick round of what passes for coffee before our call time of 10am.

After the Viper Room, we head north to Universal Studios, too busy concentrating on getting to the next location in time to appreciate that we're in LA, driving along Sunset Boulevard. We're off to film the stars of the hit sitcom, *Saved by the Bell*.

We're briefed before being allowed to enter the lot and are told not to walk across the studio floor; we must detour around it. Nor are we allowed to touch any of the equipment. And we have to get permission to set up before we start filming. The talent unions in the UK, deregulated back in the 1980s, had similar rules about crossing a shop floor. This is a salutary reminder that in the USA, studios have the power to stop us filming if one of us does the wrong thing, even by mistake.

On set, the atmosphere is calm, relaxed and above all welcoming. Once the interviews, which we film in straight takes, are done, the cast invite us to an informal lunch in the studio canteen. We have to rejig our schedule before heading back the 24 miles to Santa Monica as we haven't factored in lunch with the actors at Universal; if I had known how much time we were going to spend in the crew van getting from A to B, I would have allowed more time.

We get back to the hotel with half an hour to set up for the final shoot of the day, the highly anticipated interviews with two of the rising stars of the sitcom, *Friends*: Jennifer Aniston and Lisa Kudrow, who play the characters Rachel and Phoebe. *Friends* has only been on the air in the UK on Channel 4 since April 1995 and it is already proving to be very popular with 16–35-year-olds, the same demographic as *The Big Breakfast*'s audience. The actresses are smart, funny and completely unstarry. They both decline a make-up artist and walk in ready to do their interviews, asking for nothing more than tea and a glass of water.

At 5pm, we finish for the day. I grab all the videotapes we've recorded and am taking them back to my room when I get a call from the Executive Producer for the week. She is working through the night in the UK and is so excited about the interviews and stories we've done, she's had a change of plan.

I don't like the sound of this.

'I want to reschedule the Jackie Collins and *Friends* interviews to go out this week, not next. You'll need to send the footage down the line from an edit suite in LA, and only bring the Disneyland material back with you.'

I've already found a facilities house in West Hollywood and arranged to send some of the material on Thursday, ready for broadcast on Friday's show, so this isn't a problem. Or it shouldn't be.

'When do you need it by?'

Don't tell me: yesterday.

'If it's as good as Richard says it is and we can get it edited first thing down at the House, I'm going to put it on at 8.15.'

I have a whole seven hours, but it's evening here. I try not to panic. This is LA, a 24-hour city, so chances are that the facilities house will still be open. And the people there must be used to last-minute requests like mine, so surely a tape transfer to London won't faze them.

'Okay, I'll give them a call and get down there with the tapes. If there's any problem, I'll call you.'

'Any time. I'm here for two more hours, then I'm down at the studio for the 3.45am script meeting,' the Executive Producer says.

Once I've hung up, I punch in the number for the facilities house. Then I tell Richard and Alex I'll see them at breakfast or in the foyer at 9 the following morning. The concierge calls me a cab, but it's 5.45pm and peak rush hour. Just as the excitement of being in LA is subsiding and the jet lag is washing over me, I am once again crawling along I-10 back towards West Hollywood.

If only Anne in HR could see me now. Hardly living it up, am I?

I arrive at the facilities house, but when the Editor looks at the tapes and sees the format we've used, he tells me that they will all have to be transferred to the US system. So much for being proactive—what I didn't know is the process of sending the material to the UK automatically converts the format. Having paid over the odds to find a crew to shoot on the UK format, I could have used the US system all along. Retract that pat on the back.

What a nightmare.

'What are the chances that our Engineer in London will spot the tapes have been transferred twice?' I ask tentatively. Every transfer results in a loss of picture and sound quality.

'I bet nobody will even notice,' he replies reassuringly.

Please let's keep it as our secret.

I run into the bathroom, splash cold water on my face and tell myself to get it together. As I return to the edit suite, my phone rings. It's the Executive Producer in London. I can hear the script meeting going on in the background.

'Hello, darling. Any sign of the footage? Can't wait to see it.'

'I'm just waiting for the last transfer to go through.'

I tell myself that I made the right decision on the video tape to use with the details I had at the time. I couldn't have predicted the Executive Producer would change her mind at the last minute.

What am I talking about? They're always changing their minds. It's live television.

No excuse is going to save me if the footage is unusable.

I'll be blamed, no matter how valid my reasoning.

At least they can't fire me. Maybe there's a glimmer of hope that I can find a way out of this shit show and won't be killed the minute I set foot on British soil.

'I'll stick around here for the next half an hour while you look at the tapes, so that if we need to send them again, we can.'

'Okay, darling.'

As I get off the phone, I wipe my brow. The interviews are brilliant; Richard made sure of that. Will the footage pass quality control? I'll soon find out if it hasn't.

By now it's 8pm and I'm starving. The facilities house staff order in pizza and get me one, which is kind of them. I munch my pizza in the doorway. Then I look at my watch: it is 8.45pm.

If there was a problem, I'd have heard by now. I judge it safe to order my cab. And ten minutes later, I am zooming down the I-10 back to Santa Monica. At last, rush hour is over.

On Wednesday morning, I can't face the gym first thing. I'm exhausted from the stresses of the day before, so I tell myself I'll go after finishing the day's filming. Richard, Alex and I are due to spend the entire day at Disneyland in Anaheim, but at least I'll have the night off from transferring tapes to the UK.

After breakfast, I catch sight of Alex, Richard and the crew in the foyer, looking very pleased with themselves.

'They ran the clips on the Viper Room and *Saved by the Bell* on this morning's show,' Alex says, 'and the word from on high is that the ratings have gone through the roof. And they're expecting the same with the *Friends* interviews.'

'Fantastic news, just two more to get in the can now.' I can't admit to anyone, especially my colleagues, about the tape transfer drama. I got away with it and that's all that matters. As we pile into the van ready for the 40 mile drive out to Disneyland, I relax for a moment. I've lived to see another day.

On arrival, Richard and Alex do their best to find some funny angles on relevant stories as we film on Main Street in front of Cinderella's Castle and have photos with Mickey, Minnie, Donald and Goofy. My job is to persuade members of the public to give vox pops (informal comments) and sign release forms so that we can legally broadcast the footage.

I'm right in the thick of this when I get a call. It's the Recruitment Consultant hired by Disney, wanting to talk to me about the job at Buena Vista Productions.

She cuts straight to the chase. 'I'm putting a shortlist together before Monday of next week and I'd like to see you as soon as possible.'

Wow. This sounds promising.

'I'm in LA for work. I return to the UK on Saturday.'

'Can you meet with me on Sunday? It'll only take an hour,' she says. I can't quite believe it; I've scored an interview. But I'm right in the middle of filming and need to get her off the phone as soon as possible.

I work out that I won't get home to Liverpool until Saturday afternoon. 'I can meet you halfway between London and Liverpool on Sunday, if that suits,' I say, expecting her to say no. But before I can blink, I've arranged to meet a total stranger at a motorway service station just north of Birmingham.

As I hang up, it occurs to me it's midnight in the UK. That Recruitment Consultant certainly works some funny hours.

* * *

On Thursday morning, I head off with the team to Beverly Hills to interview Jackie Collins. Then in the afternoon, we are going to Malibu to interview comedy legend Dudley Moore. After that, I'm due back at the edit suite to transfer Jackie's tapes and send the footage to the studio in time for Friday's show.

I have hired a Make-up Artist from the same agency that

supplied our camera and sound crew. But as soon as she steps into the crew van, I regret my decision. Abbie is young and jittery; I would have preferred someone older and calmer to put our interviewees at ease.

As we crawl along the good old I-10 at 9am, barely travelling over twenty miles per hour while desperately trying not to be late for the Queen of Chick-lit, Abbie talks non-stop about how great her résumé will look with a Hollywood legend on it. Luckily, only the sound guy, Richard and I can hear her; Alex and the Cameraman are riding up front and are oblivious to what's going on in the back.

This is all I need. And what if she keeps up this fangirl bullshit when she's with Jackie Collins?

It took our Celebrity Booker months to set this up and so much is riding on it. I'm going to have to solve the Abbie problem myself before she ruins our star interview. When we pull up in the parking lot next to the bins, I jump out of the van, telling Abbie that we'll call for her when we need her. Then the team and I walk into the restaurant we have chosen for the interview and find a suitable spot.

As we are setting up, word goes round that Hollywood royalty is entering the building. Even though I've worked with tons of celebrities and am not normally the least bit star-struck, as she sweeps in, I am momentarily in awe. In all the interviews I've ever seen with Jackie Collins, she's always in full make-up and an outfit that screams Hollywood. She doesn't disappoint today.

We usher her into the empty dining room. Before Richard sits down with her, she glances at the crew, then at Alex and Richard, and finally at me.

'Can we keep it as a closed set?' she asks me. 'You don't mind, do you?'

Mind? You don't know what a favour you've just done me.

'Of course I don't mind,' I say. 'If it gets too hot in here with the lights and you need powder, we have a make-up artist on standby.'

'I've always done my own,' she says, glancing up through her false eyelashes.

'I'll be in the van with Abbie, if you need anything,' I say to Alex. Leaving him and the team to it, I head out past the bins to the staff parking lot.

As soon as Abbie sees me, she leaps out of the crew van, carrying her make-up box. She barrels towards me, a determined expression fixed on her face. I hold up a hand.

'Not so fast. Miss Collins has requested a closed set. We're both stood down.'

Abbie scrunches up her face. I half expect her to lie on the ground and beat the tarmac with her fists. Even though we are beside the bins and the smell of rotting lobster carcasses is putting me off seafood for life.

'Please, can't I just...'

'Get in the van, Abbie.'

She glares at me. 'It's not like you've ruined my life or anything.' Then she stomps back into the van and slams the door in my face. I open it again and follow her in, but the thought of being locked in a confined space with this petulant child for the rest of the day is too much. If she's going to wind me up this much, I can't have her doing the same to Dudley Moore.

'I've just got to make a call,' I say, stepping out again, call-sheet in hand as I ring his PA.

'Just to let you know that we're running to schedule and we'll be with you at two. We have a maximum of six crew, depending on whether Mr Moore requires a make-up artist.'

'Mr Moore is low-maintenance. He won't need make-up.'

Hallelujah!

'That's great. Thank you so much. We're really looking forward to meeting him and we'll see him at 2pm as arranged.'

As I put the phone down, I'm secretly doing a happy dance while trying not to give anything away. I won't risk telling Abbie yet, especially while we're alone in the van. I glance down at her make-up box as I rejoin her. Who knows what she has in there—maybe a gun? Definitely scissors. I'll pass the buck, wait until the interview is over, pull Alex aside, let him know what Dudley Moore's people have said and get him to decide on Abbie's fate.

The next twenty minutes are the longest of my life. The van is in the full glare of the sun, and even though we have the doors wide open, it's hot enough to cook an egg-white omelette on the bonnet. If it was just me, I'd go in search of coffee, but I don't trust Abbie not to hijack the interview. And I resent that even though she hasn't done any work, we'll still have to pay her fee of $1,000.

I must be in the wrong job.

Once the interview with Jackie Collins is over, the crew head back to our van. I jump out and go looking for Alex. We chat as we walk.

'I've just spoken to Dudley Moore's PA and he's not bothered about make-up. I thought we could drop Abbie off on the way if we don't need her. But it's up to you.'

'Fine with me,' Alex says as we climb into the van.

'Lunchtime?' I suggest. Enthusiastic nods all round. The Cameraman knows a great place in West Hollywood. I seize my chance.

'Isn't that where you left your car, Abbie?' I say casually. She nods. 'Uh-huh.'

'Good. We'll drop you off there as Dudley Moore's people want a closed set,' I lie.

'This can't be happening to me,' Abbie wails.

'You'll still get paid,' I mumble, shrinking back into my seat as I feel the weight of her glare piercing the back of my neck. But it's worth it. Knowing we can get rid of her and don't have to put up with her at lunchtime, I call it a win for me.

As the Cameraman fires up the engine, he calls to us in the back. 'Any music requests?'

"Ding Dong, the Witch is Dead?" No, that would be childish.

'How about "All I Wanna Do" by Sheryl Crow,' I say, the lyric about the sun coming up over Santa Monica Boulevard firmly lodged in my mind. When am I likely to be travelling this way again? Come to think of it, sooner rather than later. I still have those tapes to send down the line.

After we drop off the sulking Abbie, I relax. We have one more interview to go. As we pull up outside Dudley Moore's house, he's waiting for us at the front door—no standing on ceremony and no sign of an assistant. He shows us around, and then ushers us into a formal sitting room. There in the corner is the most beautiful grand piano I have ever seen.

We're here to talk to him about his life, and his delivery of his responses is impeccable, his wit and humour shining through. But as he was originally one half of a famous comedy duo, his eyes fill with sadness as he talks about the death of his long-term collaborator and best friend, Peter Cook. They were inseparable; losing Peter must have been like losing his right arm.

Before we know what's happening, Dudley has made his way to the piano. Did we plan this? I'm not sure. It might just be luck that the piano is in the room where we're filming. As he expresses how he feels through the medium of music, it's a moment I won't forget. I don't even know what the piece he plays is, but I could sit here all day and listen to him.

As he finishes, none of us wants to be the one to speak and break the spell. Then he stands up and bows to each side of the room, as though we're a huge audience in the Royal Albert Hall. On the drive back to the hotel, I think about what a fish out of water Dudley Moore is in LA. He's lived there for ages, but so much of what he's about seems lost in this anonymous mass of a city.

After dropping Alex and Richard off, I carry on with the crew, ready to transfer the last of the tapes. This time, everything goes without a hitch. *Phew!*

The next morning, I have an entire half a day to myself, stretching ahead of me. Our flight leaves at 4pm, which will get us back into London by coffee time on Saturday morning. I've arranged for a courier to meet me straight off the plane to take the footage from the Disneyland shoot directly to the studio, ready for editing on the Sunday night.

On Friday morning, I manage a gym visit and a swim in the outdoor pool before breakfast. But I have to put my plan to wander around the shops in Santa Monica on hold as overnight, I've received half a dozen faxes from work, all urgent. Word must have got out that I'm leaving in a week's time and suddenly every person in the office wants something from me.

Finishing everything by 11.30am, I head out the door and wander down Third Street Promenade to discover Barnes and Noble. It's a cosy, inviting bookstore that even has an area where you can sit down to read. As there's nothing like it back home in the UK, I enjoy an hour's downtime before heading to the hotel for some last-minute packing.

At check-in at the airport, I don't even bother putting

Richard forward for an upgrade. I won't impress anyone at LAX with a presenter on British breakfast television. At security, I hand over our precious video tapes to the guard, warning that they contain interview footage. Luckily, once I tell him it's Mickey and Goofy on those tapes, he treats them with the utmost respect and makes sure they get through undamaged.

This time, I've earnt that pat on the back. Not only have we pulled this shoot off, we've got some of the best interviews *The Big Breakfast* has ever broadcast.

17

When You Wish Upon a Star

London, 1995
The alarm goes off at 6am on Sunday. I've slept soundly through the night, but even though I feel rested when I wake up, I wish I had re-read my application on the flight from LA. Once I was on the Liverpool train, I was too exhausted.

After tea, a shower and breakfast, I prepare my spiel before I hit the motorway. As I drive down the M6, waves of jetlag hit me. It feels like I'm having an out-of-body experience.

Why did I agree to this? Why didn't I suggest we meet at a railway station? Then I'd have been able to focus on the interview and not on the stress of getting there alive.

Signalling to pull into the slow lane, I stay put for as long as possible before traffic from a busy slip road filters into my lane. If I can focus, I'll make it in one piece. Luckily, there are no hold ups and I arrive in plenty of time. I grab a coffee and sit in the midst of the food court area, where the Disney-appointed Recruitment Consultant, Mary, suggested we meet.

Who holds meetings at motorway service stations? Assassins? Drug dealers? Spies? Maybe Mary isn't who she claims she is and intercepted my application. Maybe I watch too many crime thrillers.

With caffeine in my system, at least I won't fall asleep during the interview or on the drive home. When Mary arrives, I assume we'll move and find a quiet corner, away from random members of the public stopping for a coffee on their way to a football match or their nan's for lunch. But no, she conducts an interview on behalf of one of the world's biggest media companies in the middle of a motorway services cafe, overheard by all and sundry. I can barely hear myself speak over the din of plates and cups rattling and excited children running up and down, but I manage to string a few coherent sentences together.

Amazingly in the circumstances, we establish a rapport. After I have answered her questions, I ask a few of my own.

Once we're done, Mary says, 'I'll be putting your name forward to senior management. Expect to hear from me soon. If all goes well, I want to line up the interviews for Monday week.' Oh the irony—my first day off after a year of breakfast television and I'll be doing the same commute. I ask her if she can schedule me after eleven as I'll be coming from Liverpool. Just over a week later, I am outside Walt Disney headquarters in West Kensington. Ros, the Executive Producer and my potential boss, interviews me. She tells me she loves *Christmas Cracker*, but stresses that she doesn't just want a production manager.

'I want someone who can take a script, polish it and run with it.'

If I'm lucky enough to be offered the job, I tell her, I'll drop everything for the chance to work at Disney. On the journey home, I can think of nothing else. I'm sure the competition is fierce, but this might just happen. I hope I don't have long to wait.

That evening, Mary rings and gives me feedback on the interview. 'Ros wants you to meet her boss. And if he likes you, then you're in.' I try not to get too excited, but unless Mary has got this wrong, this meeting sounds like a formality.

Another week passes, and then I return to West Kensington. After chatting to me for a while, Ros's boss turns to her and remarks, 'It's unanimous, I'd say.'

Ros beams at me. 'We'd like to offer you the job.'

In my mind, I imagine Jiminy Cricket singing, "When you Wish Upon a Star" and Tinkerbelle drawing the word "Disney" across a screen. I too have been touched by the brand's magic. This is my destiny. I tell Ros and her boss what an honour it is and that I can't wait to start. HR will negotiate my contract, Ros tells me. We discuss a starting date in two weeks.

Two weeks?

When I arrive home that evening, Mary calls me again.

'I didn't tell you earlier in case it put you off, but there were over 100 applications for your job. Some very experienced producers were on the short list. Congratulations.'

When the formal job offer arrives, the postie knocks on the door as the envelope from Disney is too thick to fit through the letterbox. I scan the covering letter. It's a permanent full-time contract with a three-month probationary period. The salary is more than I've ever earned in my life. The benefits are four weeks' paid holiday a year and sick leave.

And then I start reading my contract—over thirty pages of aggressively worded legalese, drawn up in the United States judging by the spelling and the tone. There are secrecy clauses about the goings on behind the scenes and relating to intellectual property, which is fairly standard. But the stipulation that employees must act as the eyes and ears of the company 24/7 goes above and beyond any normal employment contract, unless you work for MI6. Anywhere in the world, if I spot a copyright infringement, I must report the offender. Even if they're a self-employed ice-cream vendor who has the misfortune to adorn their van with badly drawn depictions of Mickey and Minnie. Oh, and this contract is "in perpetuity." To paraphrase *Toy Story*'s Buzz Lightyear, "To forever and beyond." I lie down before I sign it.

* * *

My new office is in West Kensington, on the District Line in a part of London I've never been able to afford—until now. It has parks, trees and, best of all, the River Thames. I start my house-hunt by heading south. Looking around the District Line, close to river walks, I find a one-bedroom ground-floor flat in Lichfield Court, an art-deco block on Sheen Road, that is within my budget. One of the largest blocks built in the 1930s, it has Listed Building status. The flat itself is a characterless investment property, but it is solidly built and spacious compared with modern flats. And what's more, it is ideally situated, minutes away from Richmond Station and close to the river, where I will walk or cycle before work.

Having a place I can lock up and leave when I'm on my travels is a big plus. The new job will take me away not only for location filming, but on a monthly trip to Disneyland Paris, which opened in 1992. Ros wants me to take over the monthly meetings at Disneyland Paris on her behalf as she doesn't speak French. Nor will I have to jump on the train up to Liverpool every weekend as Seán can come to London for weekends and we can explore all the lovely pubs in the area. Compared with the grittier areas of the city we've lived in together, Richmond feels like the countryside.

Marne-la-Vallée, 1995
During my first three months, my grace period, I find my feet. This time consists of planning the production slate for the year while trying to fathom the company culture. Ros flies out with me on my first trip to Disneyland Paris so that she can introduce me to my new French colleagues. At Charles de Gaulle Airport, we pick up a hire-car. I admire the way Ros merges fearlessly into the mayhem of the freeway traffic as we head southeast to Chessy, 25 miles away.

'You'll be doing this trip on your own from now on,' Ros says. I don't have any desire to drive in Paris, but I show willing and grab my notebook to write down the numbers of the freeways we're taking.

While we're in France, Ros gives me a tour of the Paris park. It's still new and shiny compared with the 50-year-old Disneyland in Anaheim, and the production design has been styled to suit the climate. One ride in particular, Jules Verne's *Rocket to the Moon*, is decorated in dark, moody colours which perfectly match the cloudy skies and frequent rain in northern France. But there is a yawning gap between the French and American Disneyland in the customer service experience. The Europeans really haven't grasped how slick American customer service is.

In the car on the way back to the airport, Ros reveals that she wants me to improve my French, and why.

'I don't know if you noticed, but every time I said something in English, they put their own spin on it in French. I could tell by their body language they were talking about us.'

'My French isn't that good. But it'll give me an incentive to work on it.'

Ros tells me that the gossip in London is about two of the French senior managers. 'They're married, but they often take their paramours out to official functions. And nobody bats an eyelid. But that's Paris for you.'

'I don't think I'll be following their example. It's hard enough keeping one relationship going.'

'All the men in London are downright envious. They wish they could get away with the same thing.'

'That doesn't surprise me.' In the London office, I hear there's an informal culture of the men socialising and playing golf together at weekends, so when a senior job comes up, it's more likely to go to one of them. It seems like there's a formidable glass ceiling that women in the company are going to need to break through. There are also some odd hires. One pretty young woman with no experience in television had an administrative job created for her by a senior male executive after he met her on a plane, according to office gossip.

I wonder what his wife thinks.

* * *

A month later, I get off my flight in Paris and head straight to the Hertz desk to collect my hire car. I've driven on the "wrong" side of the road in France many times, having been on the notorious Three Corniches in the south, along with driving around Brittany and Avignon. But for the life of me, I can't even locate my hire car in the vast multi-storey carpark where it's supposed to be parked. I walk up and down, going from floor to floor where the hire cars are parked at least half a dozen times, but keep failing to spot mine.

An hour has gone by and I am becoming increasingly anxious. Mercifully, my meeting isn't until tomorrow; I have come over a day early deliberately so that I can wander around the park on my own, familiarising myself with it. In desperation, I press the button on my car key, hoping that a random hire car will magically click open.

Come on, Tinkerbelle, help me out.

Mercifully, it works. I've never been so thankful.

I pull out my paper map, which gives me the directions and route numbers, then set off slowly, hugging the slow lane as I merge into the traffic on the freeway. At least I don't have to contend with traffic coming towards me, just speeding right up behind me and zooming into an overtaking lane at the last possible moment. I do my best to ignore the crazy driving and concentrate on taking the correct exits.

One thing I didn't do when Ros was driving was time each section of road between the exits I need. Fortunately, the signage is good and I get plenty of warning. I manage all the exits without going wrong once, even though the turnoffs are tight and the camber is at a steep angle.

An hour later, I see the signposts for Disneyland Paris. All I have to do now is find the Hotel New York. And then do all of this in reverse two days later.

When I return a month later, I am so confident I know my way, I barely need the map. I can find my way around the multi-storey car park and locate the hire car easily, so everything else should be a breeze. And this is when I screw up: I miss my turn. At the next junction, I exit the freeway and have to find the slip road to rejoin it. But because I'm coming at the junction from reverse, everything looks different.

Next time I'll take the train.

My French colleagues are wary, if not downright suspicious of their London-based counterparts. Although we grab a quick lunch together after our meetings, I sense they're only doing so out of politeness. As I remember what Ros said, it seems there is mutual distrust. It appears to be an extremely dysfunctional relationship, but maybe this is the way global corporations behave; I can't compare it with anywhere else I've worked, that's for sure. It's a relief that I have my evenings to myself to order a room-service dinner while I work through all my emails.

* * *

Madrid, 1995

Once I've got the measure of Paris, my next destination is Madrid to meet my Spanish colleagues. The Head of Production in London will be in town to oversee the recording of a music video and he's invited me along. It's an exercise in relationship building with my opposite number in Spain and to observe how the European and London Disney operations work together.

It's the first time I've been to the Spanish capital and I'm bowled over by its elegance and grandeur. We are staying in the centre at the NH Madrid Nacional, close to the Botanical Gardens and El Retiro Park, so I get up before breakfast the next morning to go for a walk. Within the park are art galleries and a seventeenth century palace. I fall in love with the atmosphere and vow to return one day with Seán.

Before I left London, Ros told me she is convinced that if the world ended between the hours of 3pm and 5pm, when our Spanish colleagues are at lunch, then it'd just be too bad. They're impossible to reach for those two hours out of the working day, but to be fair, they work as many hours as we do as they start early and finish at 7pm. Once in Madrid, I can appreciate why. The famous Spanish siesta in the big cities may be fast disappearing, but taking a break in the heat of the day seems eminently sensible to me and far more civilised than the British and American habit of working through your lunch hour, eating a miserable sandwich "al-desko."

However, adjusting to the later meal times takes practice. *Madrileños* don't really eat breakfast; or rather, the ones the Head of Production and I hang out with don't appear to. We are offered *ensaimadas*, a sugar-dusted cross between a croissant and a Danish pastry, at around 10.30am, washed down with café *cortado*: an espresso with a splash of milk. Then we work through until 2.45pm when we all troop off to a restaurant for a two-course lunch, which includes wine. The Producer of the music video and the crew come too. I don't know how they can leave a shoot for two whole hours.

After lunch, we disperse. I head to the hotel to catch up on all my faxes and emails. Sure enough, there are always urgent messages, usually from irate colleagues wondering why they aren't getting instant responses. Madrid's work culture, compared with Los Angeles and London, seems so civilised. They have their priorities right here: life first, work second. I could get used to that. Except I don't speak Spanish.

There are downsides, of course, even in this industry.

Television in Spain is partisan, and if you work for a station tied to the ruling political party of the day, you can lose your job after a general election if the opposition gets in.

I have much more success working the room in Madrid than I did at Disneyland Paris; it's a shame Spain missed out on hosting the European theme park. It has much more going for it, including a better climate. France put in a last-minute bid and lured Disney to the outskirts of the capital with a raft of financial sweeteners. As ever, money won out in the end.

After two days of lunches, dinners and a nightclub or two, it's time to return to the real world. I just hope there are more reasons for me to visit Madrid in the future.

* * *

London, 1995
I am assigned my first project on my return from Spain—the *Teacher of the Year Awards* for the Disney Channel. Ros has a Producer-Director in mind—someone who applied for my job.

This could be awkward.

But it turns out it isn't awkward at all. Once we start working together and get editorial input from senior executives who don't appear to know much about programme making, I think he's relieved he didn't get the job. One thing the various department heads are pleased with, though, is our choice of Caron Keating as Presenter. She's such a delight to work with that I forget that she's our Presenter and not one of the crew, and that perhaps I should ask her more often if she needs anything. She never does.

I recruit an Assistant Producer who, apart from being the best candidate for the job, has just the right attitude:

nothing is too much trouble. Fingers crossed she'll shake things up around here amongst the other production staff, especially all the jobsworths I've inherited. I keep out of their way and concentrate on making a programme that we can be proud of. As I'm supervising the production, I go to visit several shoots, which gives me the excuse I need to avoid the office. I visit a tough secondary school in Bristol and a delightful primary school in Enniscorthy in Ireland. Flying into Dublin in the early morning, I collect my hire car, and then spend the next hour and a half crawling through the city in rush hour.

Enniscorthy might only be 72 miles south of Dublin, but it's on a road that reminds me of rural New Zealand where it's normal to get stuck behind an elderly driver going at 30mph or, worse still, a muck spreader. Only here, there's the occasional horse or donkey for good measure. But the passing scenery of County Wexford, with trees in full leaf, is some of the most beautiful I've seen in a long time.

I arrive in the little town just as the teachers at the tiny school are spectacularly failing to keep the excited children quiet. They are sitting outdoors in a specially convened open-air assembly. The word has got around that Disney is in town. 'Miss, miss, which channel are we going to be on? BBC1, BBC2 or BBC3?' There's a burst of laughter from the assembled teachers and local dignitaries who have turned up—there is no such channel as BBC3 in 1995.

I feel sorry for the children when my team show up in normal clothes without a Mickey, Minnie, Pluto, Donald, or Goofy to be seen. Still, this is clearly something different from a normal school day. They jostle with each other for the best view and seem proud that it is their teacher who has been nominated for the award.

As we are about to start, the Head Teacher realises he's forgotten to order in the PA system.

'Could one of you fetch it from the Undertaker, by any chance?' Unusual requests being all in a day's work for me, I jump in the car. I find the Undertaker talking to the local Priest, who has just finished officiating at a funeral.

'I won't be needing it again today,' the Undertaker says, as he hands over the PA system.

'Would you mind at all if I came along to watch the filming?' the Priest asks. 'I'm done for the day, too.'

Sure, the more, the merrier.

'No, I don't mind at all.'

Our cavalcade sets off on its merry way, bumping down the tiny country roads, me at the front, the Priest following, and the Undertaker in the hearse bringing up the rear. Rather to my relief, the Undertaker turns off along the way; I can just imagine the flack I'd get if the Disney Channel found out I'd returned to the school with a hearse.

Once we wrap the shoot, we are invited to a buffet lunch. The school has gone to a lot of trouble to host us and treat us like visiting dignitaries; I only wish that I could stay on for a few days, but I'm due to return to London.

Back in Kensington, I watch a rough cut of the programme, which I show to Ros first. Then we send it over to the Disney Channel. The people there aren't happy and insist we re-edit a music track. One finalist is a special-needs teacher who we show interacting with a child with autism, but the music the Producer has chosen for this section contains lyrics questioning religion and faith. I, apparently, should have spotted the offending words.

He and I fix the problem by choosing an alternative track, but it looks like my star is falling and I've barely been with Disney three months. It may be the happiest place in the world, but it can be deeply conservative.

Just two years after we make the *Teacher of the Year Awards*, Caron Keating is diagnosed with the breast cancer that eventually takes her from all those who love her. She is just 41 when she dies.

18

Winter Wonderland

Norway, 1995

In August, Ros and I begin discussions about the filming location for the upcoming *Disney Time* to be aired on BBC1. We want snow, which can of course be faked by using machines in a studio or "doing it in post"—the special-effects process in editing which superimposes a winter wonderland courtesy of a blue-screen backdrop. But because Disney is making versions for three European broadcasters as well as the BBC, we have a decent combined budget and can afford to shoot abroad.

We settle on Scandinavia for guaranteed snow in November and choose the mountain village of Røros in Norway. A UNESCO World Heritage Site, Røros is an old copper mining town dating from 1644, and has some of the oldest and best-preserved wooden houses in Europe.

Location decided, we discuss the cartoon character guides we will feature. In Norwegian, these animated chipmunk brothers are *Snipp og Snapp,* and in English, Chip 'n' Dale. I keep it to myself, but I've never heard of them. At least chipmunks frolicking in the snow won't look quite so far-fetched as mice, ducks or dogs.

We set up a casting call for actors to play the chipmunks. At the interview, we run through the rules and responsibilities of playing the role of a Disney costume character. Most of them apply to actors at the theme parks where each costume character has a minder assigned to them, ready to pull them backstage for regular breaks. Luckily for us, we'll be working in a remote rural location on a closed set. But even so, the one golden rule that is non-negotiable is that the actors must never take their costume head off in public.

We hire two UK-based actors, recent drama-school graduates, to be our "rubber heads." It's their first ever paid acting job and they are delighted to be cast as the chipmunks, even if it is a non-speaking part. In return, they get three weeks' paid work, film on location abroad, stay in four-star accommodation, and have all their meals and travel expenses covered.

As we're filming over three weeks with four presenters, we need our Staff Production Manager to come with us. Allegra went straight from school to the BBC and, as part of her in-house training, gained some impressive accountancy skills. But this job is so much more than accounting and what I need are soft skills—a friendly demeanour, diplomacy and someone I can rely on. What I get is a frosty miss with an attitude—not what I want when we're going to be working together in the middle of nowhere in a foreign country.

When I check with Allegra about the bathroom arrangements for the presenters on location, she looks at me as though I'm a moron.

'What's wrong with going behind a tree?' she says, loftily.

I'm surprised she doesn't throw in 'They're only B-list celebrities' for good measure.

'It might be acceptable if you're a bloke, but even so, we're meant to be looking after our presenters, and this makes us look like cheapskates.'

'What do you expect me to do?' Allegra says.

Your job?

'You could find out if we can hire a Portaloo. Maybe ask a building company? They might have one spare they could lend us. When the presenters complain to us, at least we'll know we tried.'

She turns her back on me.

This will be a fun three weeks.

I fly into Oslo as part of the advanced team. At Gardermoen, I come through arrivals, where an earnest looking fellow in his mid-thirties with wild hair and standard-issue rimless glasses is holding up a sign that says "Disney Film Crew." A group of kids spot the sign, nudge each other and giggle. It's not the sort of attention we want, but as the airport is not packed like Heathrow was, I figure not many people will have noticed.

I hurry towards him. 'Hi, I'm Alison,' I say, holding out my hand.

'Hello, I'm Od.'

I can see that, but what's your name?

We shake hands awkwardly and wait for the crew. As Allegra comes over to join us, she's a different person. There's not a trace of superciliousness.

'All our equipment was offloaded at the last minute,' she says, looking at me. I shrug.

'It's a shame the airline waited until now to tell us, but we don't start filming until Wednesday. It's not the end of the world. These things happen.'

She's taken aback at my reaction.

She can't have worked on location all that much.

Although we arrived early at Heathrow to meet the crew at check-in, it took the desk at least half an hour to go through the manifest. We even saw the equipment go through the carousel, so I assumed everything was okay.

'They offloaded the kit at the last minute because of weight, but are putting it on the next flight, which gets in tomorrow morning,' Allegra says.

'It's out of our hands. Let's just get to the hotel and get something to eat.'

'Thanks for understanding,' she says. I think she means it. The following day, we return to the airport for our flight to Røros. All the equipment has arrived and is loaded on to our domestic flight, this time without mishap. We fly via Trondheim. After we've been ten minutes in the air, the coast disappears and suddenly we're flying over mountains. I look down. There are crevasses, deep fissures in the jagged peaks and the crystalline blue of long-frozen ice.

The wheels go down and we are on our final approach to Røros airport. Only, where the hell is it? It's hard to see anything as the snow is falling thick and fast. I don't see any sign of a runway. My fellow passengers—or at least, the ones who aren't part of our film crew—seem perfectly relaxed. One is still reading his book as we hit the ground. I'm not a nervous flyer except in extreme turbulence, but landing on a carpet of snow is a novel experience. Fortunately for us, the pilot must have done this a few times, as it's a textbook landing.

The drive from the airport to "town" takes ten minutes. On the way, our driver regales us with the potted history of the area. In 1644, copper was discovered in the mountains and mining was the driving force for its growth and wealth.

Once mining was abandoned in 1977, the population of Røros shrank to just over 5,000. Now, it is a mere 3,500 people.

I do a quick calculation. That's about half the number of people who lived in the nearest town to where I grew up. When I was young, I thought a population of 6,000 was the Big Smoke; my horizons have broadened somewhat since then. And then it sinks in that we're going to be spending the next three weeks in this tiny town—snowed in, by the looks of it. We'll likely have met every single inhabitant by the time we leave.

Walt Disney himself, though, couldn't have conjured up a better-looking film set. With its two principal streets full of brightly coloured wooden buildings, Røros has been lovingly cared-for and restored. Surely there must be some modern houses somewhere on the edge of town, but if there are, I don't spot them.

The townspeople can't all live here, can they?

We are staying at Vertshuset Hotel, a nineteenth-century timber building which was first a farm, and then with an additional building converted into a textile factory. The exterior is painted iron red. Inside, the factory is long gone, and in its place are hotel rooms and self-catering apartments. My apartment even has its own kitchen, kitted out with a small fridge, an electric kettle, a microwave oven, two electric hotplates and a dishwasher. The decor is warm and cosy— polished wooden floors with grey rugs and pine-clad walls. There's a dining table with four chairs, a couch, and a television.

This is to be my home from home for three weeks, so the first thing I do is kick off my shoes. The floor feels toasty warm under my toes as I pad around in my socks. As I reach down to pick up an item of clothing that fell off the hanger, I brush the floor with my hand. No wonder it's so warm—there's underfloor heating. The triple-glazed windows cut out not only the cold, but the noise too; not that there's much of that on a street which bans cars.

Once I've unpacked, I decide to explore the town to get my bearings and find the supermarket. I open one of my windows and put my hand out to test the temperature, and just as quickly withdraw it as the snowflakes melt on my palm. Work has given us all an allowance for specialist outdoor clothing for filming in extreme conditions. I decide to put all of mine on, including the ski pants.

I sit down on the step and haul on my snow boots. It's a rigmarole, this dressing for cold weather; I make a mental note to add another ten minutes to getting ready before going filming.

When I head downstairs to pick up a map, the receptionist hands me a bunch of faxes. *There's no escape, not even up a mountain in Norway.*

I glance at the faxes before stuffing them into my shopping bag; I'll deal with them later, once I've stocked up on essentials. I walk down the steps of the hotel, map in hand, head towards the crossroads and turn into Bergmannsgata, or the street of miners, which is the other main street. As the town itself is only 3.19 square kilometres (790 acres), I walk from one end to the other in fewer than fifteen minutes.

The supermarket, a Coop Mega, is only 400 metres away, which equates to a five-minute walk from the hotel, and it is huge. It's obviously the only one for miles around, as it has a large carpark. I don't need much as breakfast is included in our room deal, but I enjoy wandering around grocery shops in foreign countries, looking out for unfamiliar ingredients.

I walk around in a daze, staring at all the food items, one of which is Brunost, a caramel-coloured cheese. Although the colour is a bit off-putting, I'm game to give it a go. But what really catches my attention is the fish cabinet. It's stocked with various pickled fish, which reminds me of dissecting a dogfish in biology at school and leaving it in a jar of formaldehyde for weeks while we worked our way through the whole carcass, including the eyes. I think I'll pass on the *rakfisk*—fermented trout—as well as the fish nuggets.

Used to British supermarkets where wine and spirits are freely available, I look around to see where this one stashes its booze. I'd like to have a couple of bottles to put away for the team so that we can do a bit of bonding over a drink after work, so I enquire at the checkout, but get nothing but blank looks. This place is a long way from Oslo where English is widely spoken. The older staff struggle to understand me, so they call over a younger colleague who is fluent. He directs me to Vinmonopolet, which handily is next door. But it has a forbidding air, like I would imagine a duty-free shop in a communist country to feel, and has a very limited selection. And I don't spot any two-for-one deals either.

Vinmonopolet is the government "alcohol monopoly" agency that controls all alcohol sales in Norway, imposing a hefty tax on wines and spirits, the aim being to discourage over-consumption. What I find out later is that far from acting as a deterrent, the excess imposed spurs people on to brew their own spirits at home. When I see what the price is for a bottle of average French wine, it hits me I'd better warn the crew, otherwise everyone's per diems will disappear in a flash if they order more than one beer in the hotel bar.

I arrive back at the hotel to discover a note from a Tourist Office rep, inviting me for coffee later that afternoon. I ring her and fix the meeting for 3pm. We're due to recce our filming location, but if we go in two cars, I'll be able to make it back for my meeting as it's only a fifteen-minute drive from the hotel.

As I get into the hire car, I realise this is my first time driving on snow. The car has snow tyres, which is a relief. We leave in a convoy, and although I slide from side to side at first, it doesn't take me long to get the hang of it if I keep my speed down. I'm a dab hand at driving on the right and the roads in rural Norway are a hundred times less stressful than the urban motorways of Paris. Ours are the only cars. In both directions. For fifteen whole minutes.

The people at the front desk back at the hotel gave me a paper map to follow, but as I look around me, the only thing I can see is a snow-covered road surrounded by spruce trees. I've been warned to be careful at dawn and dusk because of the danger of hitting wildlife.

I don't fancy getting lost out here on my own. I'll either freeze to death or get eaten by a bear.

The location for the first day is a log cabin, the "home" of our two chipmunks. Surrounded by forest, the cabin is about 500 metres from the main road and only visible once we turn off. And it's here that Allegra springs an unwelcome surprise: she has made no allowance in her budget for a hair and make-up artist.

'We expect them to do their own,' she says.

'Where are they meant to do this?' I ask.

'At the hotel before we leave.'

'And between takes?'

'In the cars.'

She really knows how to treat people.

And then the penny drops: she worked in natural history before she got this job. Wildlife presenters are still mainly men who aren't known for being high-maintenance.

And I don't suppose it matters whether your face needs powdering when you're being charged by an elephant. I leave Allegra and the crew to it, offering to act as a taxi driver to ferry the presenters between the shoot and our hotel when they need the bathroom or want somewhere to reapply their makeup and do their hair.

At the briefing with the Tourist Office Representative, Bente, I run through all our locations to see if we've missed out anywhere of interest. I'm also keen to find the most reliable weather forecast, as it's only once we arrived on location that I heard the average temperatures can be wildly inaccurate. The Tourist Board, keen to lure us here, guaranteed snow, which of course is what we asked for. But in three days, we might be getting more than we bargained for as the temperature is due to drop to a lethal minus 27C. And I'm worried that the only places we can escape to between takes are the cars. While it's workable for the Presenters to run backwards and forwards to warm up, I'm worried about the Camera and Sound teams getting frostbite.

Bente has some useful advice about mealtimes, which may affect our filming schedule. People eat earlier here in rural Norway than we are used to: lunchtime is usually from 11am and dinner from 4pm. When I tell her we won't even finish filming until five, she suggests we dine in the basement bar of our hotel, which serves food until nine.

What on earth do they do with themselves in the long evenings, if they eat so early?

I return to the hotel to find that Michaela Strachan, our UK Disney Presenter, has arrived. We're filming the English version of *Disney Time* first. Michaela is best known for her work as a wildlife presenter, so is used to filming outdoors in all weathers, and she turns out to be a dream to work with.

We're all due to meet up for dinner at 7pm at Rammkjellar'n, the basement bar. In an earlier life, it was a cash vault for Røros Savings Bank and it looks like it: it has solid stone walls which look impenetrable—I doubt the bank ever got robbed—and make for highly effective soundproofing. No matter how noisy it gets down here, the sound doesn't travel and I can't hear a thing from the basement up in my room.

The next morning, it's hard to tell what time it is as it's still dark outside. I make my way to the breakfast buffet as the crew are finishing up, ready to load their equipment to be on the road by 8.30am. Allegra arranged with the hotel to deliver lunch every day at 12.30pm, but we still need to take flasks of coffee, tea and hot chocolate with us, as well as mountains of crisps, biscuits and fruit. To keep a film crew happy, you have to feed them well.

The eight of us pile into the hire cars and crew van and set off in the dawn light. When we arrive at the location at 8.45am, the sun is rising and the reindeer herder we booked is already there. The reindeer is so placid and has such a fine set of antlers, it could have walked straight off the set of *Bambi*.

Michaela is such a pro at this, we motor through the schedule. My only worry is the two young actors playing Chip 'n' Dale. Despite their furry suits, they can't wear thick thermals, otherwise their suits won't fit, so they complain of the cold, despite the gel hand warmers and hot chocolate. Between takes, the production team help them remove their costume character heads before getting them back inside the warm cars as soon as they finish their takes.

Allegra didn't manage to find a Portaloo for hire, so I put Plan B in place. My taxi service back to the hotel proves to be far more popular than I anticipated and I have to make two trips each way, using the opportunity to pick up the faxes from the office and my phone messages, returning to the apartment to deal with any urgent calls. We're expecting the German Presenter and Disney Manager to turn up soon. I get on with the German Disney Manager, but she comes from marketing, not television, and has fixed ideas on how programmes should be made. When I'm on the phone to her, I have to hold the receiver two feet away from my ear as she's so loud when she gets going with her "in Germany, we do this" spiel. It's very rare that I manage to talk her around, especially when she digs her heels in. While we're here together on location, I'm hoping we'll get to know each other better.

I get an updated message she and the Presenter are due in to Røros in the late afternoon, which gives me just enough time to dash back to the set. I drive slowly as it's getting dark. Luckily, there are no elks taking a stroll in my path. As I drive off the main road, the log cabin is lit up. The Set Designer has done a great job decorating it and it will look gorgeous on screen.

In the cabin, I discover Chip 'n' Dale, their costume heads beside them, passing a small bottle backwards and forwards, taking swigs. It could be cough medicine for all I know, but it doesn't look like it. If it's what I think it is, where the hell did they get it? They must have bought it at Heathrow Duty Free. But I'm going to have to be careful; I don't want to give them a big lecture about drinking on set if it does turn out to be cough medicine.

One of them might be coming down with a cough. But both of them?

That night in the bar, we're joined by the German Disney Manager Angela, her Presenter and Michaela, who isn't flying home until the following day. After dinner, the Director briefs the German team on the filming and I deal with all my work faxes, as well as speaking to Chip 'n'

Dale. They look at me like naughty children caught smoking behind the bike sheds, but I can't afford to alienate them—we still have many days left together on this shoot. No doubt they hate me at this moment, but they've got off lightly; *The Big Breakfast* operated a zero tolerance policy towards alcohol, other than that served at work events.

The next morning, we set off for the shoot with the German Presenter and mirror yesterday's pieces to camera. At lunchtime, I drive to the hotel with the Presenter and Angela for a pit stop. I have messages from the office and from Norwegian numbers I don't recognise.

I call Ros first. 'You've made the front pages of the newspapers, but not in a good way,' she says, her voice seething.

'What? How come?'

'See for yourself. Find a newspaper and ring me back.'

What the hell?

'I'll be two minutes. There's a newsagent round the corner.

Bye.'

Why can't she just come out with it and tell me what's going on?

I run out of my room and down the stairs, pulling on my coat, shaking. There on the newsstand is a broadsheet newspaper with a front-page photo of our shoot: an exterior shot with Chip 'n' Dale outside the log cabin, walking towards the camera. The lighting rig is set up and we're in the middle of a take. But we don't have a location stills photographer and no one asked our permission to take pictures. We're filming in a remote location and the only vehicles that came down that road have been ours. Whoever took that photo was lurking somewhere, spying.

I look at the photo more closely. It's grainy in appearance

and must have been taken with a powerful zoom lens. The photographer could be 200 metres away.

Why go to all that trouble?

And then I realise. So little happens in this tiny place that a journalist has made a story out of a non-story. They certainly went to great lengths to hide in the forest. If they're working for a national, what other paparazzo shots have they taken?

I ring Ros back.

'The photograph they've printed. Okay, they've shown behind the scenes, but it could be worse…'

'They've got interior shots,' Ros interrupts me. 'Inside the cabin, Chip 'n' Dale with their heads off. And they're drinking from a bottle. And it doesn't look like water.'

I think back to the shoot. We were filming through the open front door of the cabin for the interior shots and the lighting rig was set up to illuminate the windows from the inside. That would have given the press photographer a perfect opportunity to sneak those shots while we were so busy.

If they print that, I'm toast.

'I left the set at lunchtime as usual to drive the Presenter back to the hotel and pick up my faxes and messages. I caught Chip 'n' Dale drinking when I came back and dealt with them.'

Too late. The paparazzo creep had already got his money shot. All those phone messages from Norwegian numbers must have been journalists calling. But Ros might not throw me under the bus after all. At least, not yet.

'You need to hold a press conference,' she says. 'Whatever it takes to turn this around. I'll make sure nobody in Orlando gets to hear about it. Explain that we're filming a

Christmas special, bring Chip 'n' Dale with you. That way, the media can get their shots.'

To misquote Andy Warhol, it looks like I'm about to experience my fifteen minutes of fame.

'Wouldn't it be better to send a Disney PR representative who speaks Norwegian?'

'They don't understand TV. Here's the number of the Rep in Oslo. She'll help you organise it up in Røros. Let's do everything we can to contain this in Norway,' Ros says, before hanging up the phone.

Do the Director and Allegra know about this yet? It wouldn't surprise me if they've heard through the grapevine and not told me. But there is one person here I know I can rely on.

I punch in the number of the Tourist Office. Bente answers on the first ring.

'I'm so sorry. I saw the newspaper.'

She knows what I'm dealing with then.

'Bente, I'd love to find out how the media knew we were here.'

'Nobody from the Tourist Office told them.'

'I'm not accusing anyone. I have to organise a press conference to brief the media about what we're doing here, and I need your help. Would there be a hall I could use tomorrow evening at 6 after filming? If we schedule it for an hour, that should be enough. I know it's short notice.'

'I'll call you straight back,' she promises. I could hug her.

Fewer than five minutes later, she keeps her word and calls me. 'I've arranged it with the hotel to hold it in the conference room.'

'Thank you, Bente. For all your support.'

'It's a small town. Not much goes on. Somebody talked. I'll see what I can find out.'

'Maybe when all this is over, we could have lunch?'

'I'd like that,' Bente says. And I know she means it.

Then I ring the Disney Rep in Oslo as Ros instructed.

'Ros rang me and explained,' she says. I'm relieved I don't have to repeat the sorry tale.

'I'm planning to hold a media briefing at 6 tomorrow night in the Vertshuset Hotel. It'll be me fronting up to the media, and I'll have Chip 'n' Dale with me.'

'I'll call the Oslo press and the TV stations,' the Rep says. 'Thank you, that saves me a job,' but what the hell can I say that will keep a bunch of journalists happy? Chip 'n' Dale don't know it yet, but as it was partly their antics that got me into this mess, they're going to be the ones to get me out of it.

19

Groundhog Day

Norway, 1995
I am used to fire-fighting, but generally it's just over some production issue, not an international incident. And when the shit hit the fan before, it wasn't only down to me to sort it out.

So this is why they hired me. I was Ros's ideal candidate, remember? Maybe not anymore.

What Disney needs is a corporate PR person, skilled at handling the media and good at schmoozing. And I'm not that person.

An hour later, the PR Representative in Oslo calls me. 'There'll be ten journalists, their photographers and two news crews coming.'

I'll be on the six o'clock news and in the newspapers? Are you kidding?

'And a journalist wants to interview you live on breakfast radio tomorrow morning at 8.30.'

I've always been behind the camera, away from the limelight.

When will this be over?

'Why are they making such a big deal of this? I know not much happens in a small town, but...'

'They think Hollywood has come to Røros and that something bigger than *Disney Time* is going on. They think you're here making a feature film.'

'Then they'll be very disappointed.' It's a children's cartoon show, not the latest *James Bond* movie. No matter what I tell them, I guess the media will print anything they like. And I won't even be able to read the story as it'll be in Norwegian. But then, neither will my boss. I just have to make it through the next 24 hours.

I scribble down some notes about the programme content and the countries taking part, as well as information about the clips. I'll introduce Chip 'n' Dale, remembering to call them Snipp and Snapp for the Norwegian journalists, and then take questions. What else can I tell them?

While people with real jobs are saving lives, educating, questioning suspects, I'm getting wound up over a media conference about chipmunks. I wonder what Mum would have told her competitive friends if they'd asked her what I was doing right now.

'She works for a mouse. And now she's filming in Scandinavia with chipmunks.'

'Chipmunks? Real ones? With David Attenborough?'

'I expect so.'

* * *

I do the radio interview as I walk up the snow-covered slope towards the set location. The presenter is wildly enthusiastic and a huge Disney fan, so it comes across as a conversation with no awkward silences or tough questions.

See, you can do this.

I call the PR Rep afterwards and ask if she can obtain a copy of the recording to give to Ros. Then I spend the rest of the day fretting about the media conference and photo call. Ten journalists!

I try not to stare directly into the lenses of the two television news cameras trained on me. But the flashes on the stills cameras unnerve me.

This will soon be over. Nobody in the UK will see it and I'll survive.

I do my spiel about *Disney Time,* and then call my support act, Chip 'n' Dale, who are hiding in the wings.

'Ladies and Gentleman, let me introduce you to Snipp (Chip) and Snapp (Dale).'

As they shuffle forward, a journalist asks, 'And which is which?'

Floor, swallow me now.

I turn to the chipmunks, forgetting they aren't allowed to talk.

Their teeth are different. Chip has teeth joined together, Dale has two separate ones. Or is it the other way around?

'Step forward, Chip... umm, sorry, I mean Snipp.'

As Snipp (Chip) lumbers towards me, it turns out she is the one with the black nose. That's how you tell—Dale's (Snapp's if you're Norwegian) is red.

Why didn't I learn that?

The girls nod and wave at the assembled media reps. A journalist even cracks a smile. The others don't. I can't put this off any longer.

'I'll take your questions now.'

'Which would you say is your favourite?'

I could kill them both right now. They helped put me in this mess.

But I'm not being entirely fair. The only "Chip 'n' Dales" I'd heard of before this shoot were the cheeky male strippers. And I've certainly never watched a *Chip 'n' Dale* cartoon, so the notion that these two have unique characteristics has so far escaped me.

'I can't choose. I wouldn't want to upset either of them.'

No more than I have already.

As I suspect, the journalists didn't fly all the way up from Oslo to talk about cartoon chipmunks. When one asks a question about Disney in LA buying up another film company, I shut him down. That one is way over my pay grade.

'I suggest you speak to our PR Rep in Oslo about that. Thank you all for coming.'

From the looks of disappointment on their faces, I realise they're not looking forward to telling their editors that Disney isn't in Røros to make a big Hollywood movie, despite the rumour mill working overtime. All we're doing is making *Disney Time* Christmas specials for the European Head Office in London. Not even Los Angeles.

When the stories come out the next day, I don't bother getting them translated. What went on in Norway will stay in Norway.

Although we suspect that the paparazzo photographer who rumbled us flew back to Oslo with his colleagues, we can no longer afford to take any chances on set with the chipmunk characters. The girls still take their costume heads off inside the log cabin between takes, but only when the curtains are drawn. When they go outside, they have to be in full costume, apart from when they're getting in and out of cars to and from the set. Even then, we are careful that nobody else is around to witness it. That is easy to do at our remote set location, less so in the carpark in Røros.

With the drama of the press intrusion out of the way, I can get on with making the actual programmes. But just imagine if Allegra had had her way. Chip 'n' Dale would have been going to the loo behind a spruce tree instead of back in their rooms at the hotel. What if the photographer had caught that?

* * *

The nearest gym is in the town's big hotel, but I don't get to it very often, so in my rare downtime, I set off on a hike in the snow for some exercise. I start to feel nervous once I leave the town. If there are footpaths, they're invisible in this white-out. My boots sink into the soft powder. Each step is an effort. And there are no landmarks in the forest—one snow-covered pine tree looks very much like the next. If I become lost, I'll never find my way back. I turn around to look back the way I have come; my tracks have all but disappeared in the short time I've been walking. The twinkling lights of Røros have never looked so welcoming.

Ten days into the shoot, the mercury plummets and it gets dark at 3pm. I learn to associate bright sunshine and cloudless skies with weather better suited to polar bears. When the mercury dips to minus 26, I take Allegra aside to suggest we have a rest day and work on a weekend day to make up for lost time. She's adamant that we must carry on now, because if we follow my suggestion, the Crew won't get a proper two-day break. I moot that we ask the Crew what they'd prefer, but Allegra's hackles are up. Her body language screams, 'Ask the Crew? Are you mad?'

It's not my responsibility to run the shoot, but when the Film Crew isn't being looked after properly, I weigh in. And when the Sound Operator's fingers seize up in the bitter cold, I remind Allegra that she'd better check our insurance cover. But the Nordic weather gods turn out to be on our side as for the next few days, there is cloud cover and the temperature stays a balmy minus 7. The sound guy keeps all his fingers.

* * *

Every day, I get up and drive between the hotel and the set location, seeing a snow-clad pine forest and two chipmunks. I call it my *Groundhog Day* routine; all I need is to wake up to the strains of 'I Got You Babe' for the image to be complete. Then, just like the movie, one day, something different finally happens. My phone rings while I'm en route. I pull over and come to a sliding stop.

It's Ros. 'Something's come up. I need you in Orlando by the end of the week.'

Orlando as in Florida? Where it's hot?

'Yes, of course. I'll be happy to go.' *Happy? I'll be ecstatic to get out of here.*

'Mike's going to be filming at the park for the Disney Channel *Christmas Special* and we want better footage than the usual. The two of you will come up with something more imaginative, I'm sure. I'll hand you over to Rachel to organise your travel.'

As I run through the itinerary with Rachel, reality starts to sink in. Today is my last day in Røros. Tomorrow, I'll fly out at midday for a connecting flight to London. I'll have 24 hours at home to unpack my winter gear, do laundry, pack a bag of summer clothes, run around and do any last-minute shopping before my flight on Thursday.

I drive off to the set location, barely able to contain

myself. Half a dozen forlorn figures stand around in what appears to be a blizzard. I go up to Allegra.

'You're doing such a good job that I plan to leave you to it.' She arches one eyebrow. It's not quite a withering look, but close.

'Really?'

'Ros wants me in Orlando. My flight out is tomorrow.'

'That's a shame. We'll miss you.'

Oh, sure.

'Unless there's anything else you need, I'd better go. Bags to pack and goodbyes to say. I'll pick you up after the shoot.' I drive back down the snow-covered country road between mile upon mile of pine forest, superimposing tropical sunshine and palm trees over the image and singing 'I Got You Babe' with a touch of irony. For me, *Groundhog Day* is well and truly over.

I treat all the team to a celebratory goodbye drink on this, my last night, putting it on to the company credit card, even though Accounts will give me a hard time. For nine drinks, mostly beers, the bill comes to over a hundred pounds. Wine is twelve pounds a glass.

Next day at the airport—the smallest one in the world to be served by a jet, the locals proudly tell me—the Head of the Tourist Board himself is there to see me off. He hands me a gift, a token of the town. A small flute-like instrument, it looks like a Norwegian version of the recorder. And he bestows me with the freedom of the town. I'm quite overcome by his kindness.

As I bid him farewell, thanking him for all his help, I'm distracted by the deteriorating weather. A blizzard blankets the runway. It doesn't look promising. The incoming plane lands on what looks like solid ice.

I shut my eyes as we rumble down what must have once been tarmac and sigh with relief as we lift off over the frozen landscape. After dropping into Trondheim, I resume my journey south. In the hour we're in the air, we pass no other signs of human habitation. When the plane approaches Oslo, after Røros, it looks as lively from the air as an Istanbul bazaar.

20

The Truman Show

Orlando, Florida

I arrive home late that night and spend the following day racing around, getting everything ready for Florida. Before I knew I was going to Orlando, I'd arranged to go out as soon as I was back in the UK with a colleague who is a reliable source of office gossip. We'd intended meeting for a quick catch-up, but I find it such a relief to be back in the big city with fun company, it turns into dinner—with drinks. Lots of them.

I wake up the following morning feeling very peculiar when the alarm goes off at six. The flight doesn't leave until lunchtime, but instead of the fifteen-minute taxi ride from Kew to Heathrow, I allow an hour to get to Gatwick. Pitched to passengers as London's other airport, Gatwick is nothing of the sort; it's in Sussex and much nearer to Brighton and the coast than London. Check-in is at 10.30am, so pick up is 9.30, allowing for the limo service to collect me from outside East Sheen Waitrose rather than the Richmond one, where I actually live. This service has a knack of only being late when it really counts—when I'm racing to do an online edit, or catch a transatlantic flight.

On the seemingly endless car journey, my stomach and headache merge into the mother of all hangovers. By sheer force of will, I manage not to throw up in the back of the limo. I grab a bottle of mineral water and gulp half of it down as I queue for check-in. I'm the last passenger, which is a bad sign. Then, to my surprise, I'm upgraded from Premium Economy to Upper Class.

I rush off to the satellite, which is another word for the furthest point in the entire terminal, stroll straight on through the front door of the plane and sit down. Nobody checks my ticket, but as I settle in, a crew member hands me a glass of champagne. This is the last thing I need, but I take a sip, anyway.

I look up at the flight information: London Gatwick to New York JFK, flight time seven hours, thirty-five minutes. Seriously? I bolt from my seat, grab my carry-on from the overhead locker and rush out to the adjacent gate, where a crew member on the Virgin flight to Orlando is just about to close the door.

I sit next to a retired teacher from Oxford who is going to spend Christmas with her family in Tallahassee. She's a first-timer to most forms of technology and I spend a good deal of the flight answering her questions.

'Can you tell me, dear, how I recline my seat? Is the news that we're watching live or recorded? Can I make a phone call or would that be showing off?'

Ten hours later, she's a technology whizz and I'm exhausted. We're circling the Magic Kingdom, where the golf course is carved into the shape of Mickey's face. While the other passengers marvel at how cute it looks, to me, coming here for work and already exhausted, it seems that Mickey will be watching my every move, now that I've swapped the wilds of Norway for three weeks in "the happiest place on earth."

One of the three minders assigned to the shoot collects me from the airport, looking like a cross between a Mormon missionary and a GI. As their purpose is to prevent the UK team from filming anything we shouldn't, I nickname him and his colleagues the Secret Service. Even Disney employees can't be trusted, apparently. Or at least, not the ones based in England.

He drops me off at the Walt Disney Beach Resort, where our crew is staying. As I get out of the car, the doorman—a resting actor, judging by the way he hams it up—greets me with, 'It costs nothing to smile.'

You'd look like this too, sunshine, if you'd just flown for ten hours with a banging hangover after three weeks up a mountain.

I restrain myself from running over his foot with the luggage trolley for his passive-aggressive comment.

'You have a nice day too,' I reply, but I think irony is wasted on him.

The theme of this hotel is New England Yacht Club and my room is decked out like a suite on a fancy yacht. I can scarcely believe the opulence after my humble log cabin room in Røros. All I want to do is have a shower and crash out for a couple of hours, but I feel a nagging anxiety to plug in my laptop and download my messages before I do anything else. There were seven phone messages waiting for me as I checked in, from London and Norway. I check the time difference: it's mid-afternoon here, 8.30pm in London and 9.30pm in Norway.

The call from Allegra I deal with by email and the other

six can wait until tomorrow when colleagues are in the office. But of course, as soon as I upload my messages, 23 others appear in my in-box. They too can wait. I turn away from my computer and look out my window. In front of me is the most beautiful free-form swimming pool I have ever seen; I opt to shower poolside.

I fling open my suitcase and rummage through it. My swimmers are at the bottom of the case. Typical. I put them on, noting how ridiculously white and blotchy my sun-starved skin looks. To hell with it.

Not only is it the most beautiful hotel pool I've ever swum in, there's no nasty chlorine smell as the staff use fresh water and heat treat it. After a quick swim and another shower back in my room, I feel refreshed. So much for catching up on sleep. I message Jenna, the Production Manager, and suggest we all meet for a drink and an earlyish dinner together this evening. If I pace myself, I could keep going until about 9pm before I conk out and fall over like the mechanical pink toy on TV battery advertisements.

For this Christmas special, I've brought in Mike, who I've worked with before. I recruited Jenna after she applied for the *Teacher of the Year* post. She isn't that experienced, but she's very smart. It's a joy to be among friends and I never need to watch my back with these two.

The Secret Service, though, are another matter entirely. Mike, Jenna and I share intelligence on how we'll manage them. Their official title is Disney Parks Liaison Officers, their job to accompany film crews around the park. From the footage we saw before coming out to Orlando, we know most of the material shot under their watch has been generic stuff for US broadcasters and of such poor quality, it wouldn't pass muster in the UK—British audiences aren't so easily fobbed off. We're working on a commission for the Disney Channel to make a Christmas Special to be broadcast to the UK and Europe. And while our minders think that we'll be content with filming the Christmas Parade and some out-of-tune Disney employees dressed as elves singing carols, we have other ideas.

Our evening stretches out until 9.30pm and I'm sparked out by 10. At 4.30 the next morning, I'm woken up by a phone call. My first thought is that there's been a crisis, but it's Rachel—Ros and my PA—who says she's just hooking me up for a conference call. What conference call? Why on earth does anyone think they'll get anything sensible out of me, given the ungodly hour?

I grab my laptop while we're talking and see for myself. Sure enough, there in the diary is our monthly status meeting. It appears all my colleagues are gathered in the boardroom, waiting for me to join them. I'm greeted by our Head of Production. He's nice enough, but his Assistant has been sending me pithy emails for the past couple of months. I've barely been in the office and thought I was well away from office politics. Not so. Although I can't see her as the conference call is audio only, I imagine her biding her time.

I'm not wrong. When I can't answer her list of questions, she's ready to stick the knife in. If it was that important, I think, why couldn't she have sent them over by email first? If it wasn't 4.30am where I am, I might have had the information to hand, I say. It isn't her problem, she implies, and the team wants an answer straight away.

Note to self: *turn your phone off at night in future*. No, that wouldn't work. They'd only call me via the switchboard. I get up as soon as the call is over and spend the following hour trying to get her off my back. Which I do—for now.

Over breakfast, Mike, Jenna and I cook up a strategy to

become chummy with the Secret Service by finding areas of common interest. They play golf, which is lucky as Mike does, too. They like rock of the head-banger variety and have never heard of indie music, much to Jenna's amusement. The youngest and best looking of the trio is rather smitten with her, but as he's also the most junior, we aren't able to use that to our advantage.

We decide to humour them by filming the Disney Parade and the singing, knowing we will have to tweak the footage, especially the sound, in post-production. When we finalise the sound edit, Mike replaces the tuneless Disney elves with a music track from Cambridge's King's College Choir. An on-the-ball Disney Channel executive queries why the singing is so good; I can guess what he's thinking.

You're taking the piss.

Yes, we are, but you'd complain a whole lot more if we included the original version.

In return for doing what the Secret Service want, we propose a piece on the Imagineering Department, where the theme park rides are designed. They're reluctant, questioning what imagineering has to do with Christmas. Nothing. But we're short of material as most of what we've been promised has turned out to be unusable.

Luckily, 1995 is the first year that an entire street's spectacular Christmas light show has been recreated at Walt Disney World. It's the brainchild of Jennings Osborne from Arkansas, who displayed it outside his home for years until the neighbours complained about all the visitors clogging their street. Osborne's solution was to donate the light show to Disney. Not only does the footage look great on camera, but our viewers will be the first in the UK to see it.

The compelling Disney stories are the ones the Secret Service will never give us permission to film. But during our shoot, Ros comes to the park with another programme idea, this time about Celebration, the utopian village where people would live and work that was the pet project of Walt himself. In 1994, some 38 years since Walt's passing, Disney revived the project to sell as an idealised vision of what a community should be. And the prospect was so enticing that 5,000 people entered a lottery to compete for 474 houses. We're keen to talk to the buyers, interested to know who they are and whether the town is only for diehard Disney fans or attracts others to the promise of life in a place fuelled by nostalgia. The Secret Service give us a quick tour of what's been built, but then, without warning, the shutters go down and Disney axes our project.

Of course, we then think the company is hiding something. We may be Disney employees, but we're storytellers too, so we can't resist doing a little digging, despite being told to back off. One of the more bizarre aspects of Celebration concerns the control the company has over the homeowners. Residents can choose from six house designs, but everything else has to conform, right down to the plants in the garden.

After ten days at Walt Disney World, I feel like I too am living in an alternative reality. Every time I step into the lift, the recorded music is "It's a Small World (After All)." Then I notice the toilet paper in the bathrooms is embossed with the face of Mickey Mouse. When I go for a walk past a golf course on Disney property, I see a weird scaly creature the size of a badger. Dismissing the idea that this is a hallucination that I can no longer put down to jetlag, I assume it must be some sort of animatronic. If Disney has gone to all the trouble of creating a golf course in the shape of Mickey Mouse's ears, robotic animals to amuse golfers can't be that far-fetched, can they? The creature turns out to be a real live armadillo. They're common in Florida, but to my eyes, this one is as other-worldly as a baby dinosaur.

Another dinosaur-like creature that inhabits the wilder parts of Walt Disney World is not only real, but lethal if you're unlucky enough to encounter one. On our last night in Orlando, the Secret Service take me, Mike and Jenna out for a farewell dinner and on to a nightclub afterwards. After a couple of drinks, they loosen up a bit and spill the beans on some stories (real or imagined) that swirl around the theme park.

Walt decided to build the park in the 1960s on what the sellers considered to be swampland. In 1967, as the park was nearing completion, the landscape design ensured that lakes, many of which were man made, connected the resorts by a series of canals. At this time, the American alligator was declared an endangered species and given federal protection.

And all those lakes around the resorts, according to the Secret Service, harbour a healthy alligator population.

'And how do the 'gators get from lake to lake?' I ask.

'Via the canals, of course.'

You can paddle a canoe around the lakes, we're told, but are advised to keep away from the uninhabited islands, where there are discreet signs warning paddlers from landing. Whether the Secret Service guys are trying to scare the visiting crew over from England, I don't know, but as they walk us back to our hotel after our night out, they take us on a detour to a bridge over the Seven Seas Lagoon and recount a tale of a Disney employee who allegedly jumped into the lake from that bridge for a dare. He was never seen again.

But it isn't the local wildlife that scares me; it's the increasingly toxic corporate culture. It hasn't taken me long to figure out where I fit in within the Disney hierarchy.

Disney London and Europe don't really count on this side of the pond; when we try to make culturally specific content, it's generally vetoed by a PR machine. It seems my colleagues in LA won't countenance the idea that anything made in Europe could be worth watching.

21

The Hunchback of Notre Dame

London, 1996
I spend a lot of time living out of a suitcase and long to find a more permanent place in London. While in Norway and the USA, I put an offer in on a flat in Kew. Marketed as a "garden flat," in reality, it's the ground floor of a Victorian railway cottage on North Avenue with a sunless patch of dirt out the back. But not only is Kew more affordable than Richmond, it's also closer to work.

When I give my notice to my landlord, he holds on to part of my bond as he claims the oven wasn't cleaned properly. I was never there to use it, but there's no disputes resolution service for tenants to complain to and no way to recoup the unreasonable amount of money he withholds. I cut my losses and look forward to moving into my own place. I love the area, with all the restaurants and cafes within walking distance, as well as Kew Gardens and the Thames.

Before I bought the flat, I knew the street would be noisy. The only reason I'm able to afford it is because it is next to the District Line Tube, which runs above ground rather than below, so I factored in that the first Tube of the day runs at 4.45am and the last at midnight. But what only becomes apparent after I move in is the constant assault from the skies; Kew is on the flight path into Heathrow. If the Tube doesn't wake me up, the early morning flights coming into land do. As I lie there, wide awake long before dawn, I imagine anxious and excited passengers. A bit like me when I first left home and flew across the world, ready to start a new life.

As I know I'll be woken up very early, I try to get to bed by 11pm. But this doesn't work either. My upstairs neighbour is friendly and sociable—too sociable—and she and her boyfriend like to party, even on school nights. I put up with it at first as he only comes over a couple of nights a week, but when the guitar comes out and he sings—or rather, bellows at the top of his tuneless voice—it starts to become too much.

Then he moves in full-time. The first thing he does when he takes up residence is to remove all the sound insulation between the two floors—namely the rugs and carpets. As we don't own the freehold to the house, he is in breach of the lease by doing this, but I feel too intimidated to complain to the freeholder as I don't want to fall out with the neighbours. But in between the shouting and laughter at their loud dinner parties, all I hear is the constant scraping of dining room chairs against the bare floorboards. The lack of sleep and demands of my job combine to drag me down.

At work, I notice a difference in the behaviour of the Head of Production's frosty Assistant, Sally. Whenever she wants something, she'll bowl into my office unannounced and shut the door behind her to interrogate me alone. She's clearly trying to wield her power over me, and at first it works as I find her tactics increasingly threatening. Then I wise up to her methods and pointedly get up from my desk, opening the door she's just closed and telling her I'm busy and I'll get back to her.

In the television industry, calling out a bully is tantamount to signing your own professional death warrant. I can forget going to Inhuman Resources, as I call HR, who protect the company, not the employee. I could complain to my boss, but I don't expect a sympathetic hearing. So at work, I keep quiet about Sally's behaviour and seek help from an outside counsellor. But as she's had no experience in a toxic corporate work culture, there's little point in continuing. Instead, I ride it out and hope the problem will go away.

But being seriously undermined by someone wanting to trip me up at every turn is unnerving, particularly when coupled with sleepless nights at home. It doesn't take long for nagging self-doubt to seize control. I'm in a meeting with a Producer-Director team, going over the script for *The Making of 101 Dalmatians*, when I have a panic attack in the middle of giving feedback.

Who do I think I am? Surely they'll see through me. I'm just a country kid who loves to ride horses. I don't belong here. Maybe I should go back to where I came from. But where the hell is that? Malaysia? Sussex? New Zealand?

I excuse myself from the meeting, run off to the bathroom and take a long hard look at myself in the mirror.

You survived ten hours of live television a week. Don't give up now.

I return to the meeting as though nothing has happened and carry on where I left off. I'd let a bully get to me. It won't happen again.

By this time, I have something more pressing to concern me and that's the contract to deliver the completed 52-minute *The Making of the Hunchback of Notre Dame* documentary. Two weeks after filming at the Eurostar terminal at Waterloo, as instructed by my nemesis in Film Marketing, I get another call from the two-headed monster that is Scimogen.

'Guys, the Eurostar promotion got nil points from LA, so no can do, okay?'

'We wasted half a day filming at the busiest station in Europe, paid a film crew for a whole day and can't use any of the footage in the documentary?' I say with as much sarcasm as I can muster.

'You know it.'

We don't yet have a workable structure for the documentary, nor do we have a story. The clock is ticking down and the money is running out. Stephen and I travel to Paris to interview the French animators who made the opening sequence and film at Notre-Dame, then on to Chartres and Reims cathedrals for more gargoyles. We film jousting and a bird of prey display at a medieval festival in Provins, 40 miles outside of Paris. Adding in the clips from the film we've been told we can use, we send off the rough cut for approval.

We don't have to wait long. I receive an email from Feature Animation in LA that begins with the words "I'm not comfortable with" and proceeds to rip the rough draft to shreds. The language is measured, but the tone is menacing. What the Feature Animation people dislike the most is the use of the mime artist to represent Clopin—the same Clopin that my boss suggested we link the documentary with in the first place—and complain that the stop-start links interrupt the flow of the story.

I re-read the email half a dozen times. The upshot is that Feature Animation in LA hate the rough draft of our film with a passion and express that hate with a fury that astonishes me.

Victor Hugo's *Hunchback of Notre-Dame* is a classic dark novel. Why anyone at Disney thought it was culturally appropriate to take this masterpiece of French literature and turn it into an animated feature comedy suitable for children, I'll never know. We are ordered to remove all the dark elements from our promotional film, particularly the inciting incident where Quasimodo's mother is killed on the steps of Notre-Dame by the evil Frollo (a sexual predator if ever there was one). Dark doesn't equal bums on seats, apparently, even though this scene is in the actual film. And you don't need to be a parent to realise that the subject matter isn't exactly suitable for young children.

What this teaches me is that a film made by an interfering committee never works. But what it doesn't do is solve my immediate problem of making a documentary that will appease my corporate masters and be acceptable to the TV channel funding the project. It's crunch time. If I don't deliver a finished programme, I'll never eat lunch in this town again. I'll never eat lunch in any town. Not even Tanjung Malim or Motueka.

At the weekend, I mull over what to do and come to the conclusion that to salvage my career, I must replace the Director. Before I talk to Ros, I sound Mike out to see if he's available at the eleventh hour. He's keen, but is going away on holiday in three days and I'll have to finish the film myself, if necessary. I consult Ros, and then have to tell Stephen. It's brutal, but it's either my job or his on the line. And I have a lot more to lose.

Mike and I barely see daylight for the following thirty-six hours as we put in sixteen-hour days in the edit suite while the clock ticks down. We come up with a new structure and decide to pull the whole thing together using voiceover. We still have to write that, but I've always loved a deadline and I'm doing what I do best: putting together a story while cocooned from toxic office politics. Luckily, our first choice of voiceover artist, Ardal O'Hanlon—Father Dougal in the hit comedy *Father Ted*—rejigs his schedule and manages to squeeze this job in.

While I'm frantically editing *The Making of the Hunchback of Notre-Dame*, all my Disney colleagues are away on a three-day team-building exercise. I can think of nothing worse than pretending to cosy up with people who just want to stab me in the back, so I stay away, using the documentary as an excuse. But the Disney masters aren't having a bar of it and summon me down to Egham. I agree to go for one evening after the edit to attend dinner, stay the night, and then be released so that I can finish the programme.

I frock up and leave the edit suite in Soho at 6.30pm before hailing a cab and crawling out of central London to get to the Runnymede on Thames Hotel and Spa in Egham. As I walk into the dining room, they're all sitting there, my colleagues, waiting for me. All eyes are on me, including Sally's. My first instinct is to run away, but I have to play the game. As soon as I sit down at the table, my boss briefs me.

'We want you to tell us what you consider your finest achievement.'

The thing I'm most proud of is being part of a class-action committee of bereaved families. We won that momentous court case against British Rail to improve train safety and install central locking on intercity trains after Mum and hundreds of other victims had fallen to their deaths. But I don't tell them that.

'My finest achievement at Disney is giving people jobs and delivering the *Making of* programme,' I gabble.

Can I go and finish that now?

Against all odds, not only do I get a worthy *Making of The Hunchback* programme out on time, it achieves high ratings. Even the *Daily Mail* newspaper likes the programme and gives it four stars.

In August 1996, mission accomplished, I'm called into Ros's office where she asks me if I'm happy.

'No,' I tell her bluntly. 'I am not happy with how Feature Animation in LA was so brutal about the rough cut. Stephen's lack of television experience and inability to work under pressure didn't help.'

She tells me I should have said something earlier. But as he is a friend of hers and she'd already hired him, it was too late.

'It wasn't ideal to bring in Mike so late, but I'm proud of the end result, which is all that matters, isn't it? The viewers liked it, so did the critics.'

'The trouble with you is that you have never been injected with the Disney microchip, which is what I like about you,' Ros says. I laugh. I learned as a seven-year-old at boarding school that the only way to cope with being institutionalised is to pretend I am not there and retreat into my imagination.

'I can't see you dressed up as a costume character in a parade on Main Street, either,' she says, referring to an initiation rite at Disney where senior executives have to do exactly that—in front of the paying public. When I first heard this, I refused to believe it. Ros assures me it's true and tells me the story of a senior manager dressed as Pooh Bear in a heatwave. His minder, who was meant to monitor how long he could spend in a furry suit without suffocating, was clearly having an off-day; a near-delirious Pooh Bear had to be rescued and pulled backstage before he passed out and needed CPR. Not exactly a good advertisement for the "happiest place on earth."

'Over my dead body,' I retort. 'After three weeks at Walt Disney World, I can't say I love theme parks.' There, I've said it. I didn't even like Disney cartoons as a kid; I preferred the antics of Daffy Duck, Porky Pig, Sylvester the Cat and Tweety Pie, made by the opposition, Warner Brothers.

'What do you want to do?' Ros asks.

'Make the most creative programmes possible without the constant nitpicking and editorial interference from all the vested interests, who keep shifting the goalposts. None of them have any clue about programme making.'

It's clear to both of us I'm not cut out for the corporate world. Nor am I interested in schmoozing, gaming the system, or climbing my way to the top. And even though I have my own place, either Seán or I still have to travel at weekends if I'm ever to see my beloved.

'Let me know what you decide about your future and we'll take it from there,' Ros says.

After yet another disturbed night, listening to the upstairs neighbours partying while I long for sleep, I go to work the next morning and hand in my notice. I speak to a few estate agents about renting out the flat. The rent should just about cover my mortgage.

Disney gives me a month's salary. I'd get more if the company made me redundant or fired me, but as it has no grounds for either and I've resigned voluntarily, this is the best I can hope for. I think it is what Ros wanted all along. She led me to believe I'd have autonomy, but when it really mattered, I didn't.

My leaving do is lunch at the River Cafe in Hammersmith. It has an open kitchen and we watch the chefs as they work. A young sous-chef with a mop of blond hair and a loveably mischievous air about him catches my eyes as he's plating up. I like to think now that it was a fitting farewell to my time in London to have lunch cooked by none other than the Naked Chef, Jamie Oliver.

22

Shameless

Liverpool, 1996–2000
Only once I'm back home do I realise the effect long-distance commuting has had on me. I felt so guilty about the two years I spent at film school that I fixated on recouping my lost earnings. Even though I have *The Big Breakfast* and Disney on my CV, I'm looking outside of London where there are fewer TV jobs, so my search becomes both easier and more difficult.

I talk my way into a storylining workshop on the long-running TV soap *Coronation Street* with eight other screenwriters, all of whom are more experienced than me. We are invited to pitch our ideas to established storyliners and writers, and then to submit our written storylines. Although I'm not offered a contract, the Producer tells me he'll recommend me when there's a vacancy in Production Management. A sensible person would have leapt at that, but I didn't attend film school to go back to what I was doing before. I tell him I'll consider it. A year after saying goodbye to the weekly commute, I'm working part time as a lecturer in screenwriting at Liverpool's John Moores University.

During a phone call with my sister, she mentions her concern over a puppy in a litter of pedigree Labradors. The pup is nearly three months old, but yet to find a home. If I was thinking of getting a dog, this one would be "the one," but if you work in television, you never know for sure when you'll get home each evening. I can't be relied upon to look after a cat, let alone a dog.

But I make my decision with my heart, not my head. And it takes all of thirty seconds. I don't even consult Seán. I'm taking on a commitment which will affect my working life, but I don't care. And I've chosen a large breed of dog who will need two decent walks a day, even though I know full well that when I get another television job, it's likely to be based in Manchester. And what's more, we live in a maisonette with three floors, a shared front garden and a balcony. But across the road from our flat is woodland, ideal for dog walking.

We could always hire a dog sitter.

It takes nine hours for me to drive to Devon that weekend as there are snarl-ups in Birmingham, Bristol and Exeter. And the return journey north on the Sunday takes just as long—not because of the traffic, but because sitting in the footwell of the passenger seat, safely wrapped up, is the dearest little black Labrador puppy called Zebedee with the softest paws imaginable. I stop at nearly every service station to give her a comfort break and a little walk.

My income from part-time university teaching works out at less than minimum wage because I spend hours preparing and marking. But I had to accept a contract on a per-hour basis and only get paid for the contact hours with the students, even though I have an MA and a ton of industry experience. The university is lucky to have me.

I last for two semesters, but turn down any future offers

of teaching unless the university offers to pay me properly. Fortunately, I hung on to my flat in Kew, which should give me a good return on my investment one day. When my first set of tenants moves out and I need to re-decorate before re-letting, I decide to take Zebedee with me. Although there isn't any green space in my noisy little street in London, the river and the towpath aren't all that far away.

Heading down south on the M40 with vacuum cleaner, mop, brush, cleaning equipment and dog, I amuse myself by thinking about my ex-colleagues at Disney. If only they could see me now in my latest role as landlady and dog owner. I love going back to Kew on my own terms, not beholden to my corporate masters.

While I paint and re-decorate, Zebedee sits chewing on a toy, rolling on the carpet, or waiting patiently for me to scratch her tummy. She's delightful company. I give myself three days to do the work. On our last morning, we wake up early and go for a walk along the river. Heads down, harried commuters make their way towards Kew Station. I'm grateful I'm no longer one of them.

When we return from our walk, I grab some toast, give Zebedee her breakfast, and then do a last clean before locking up. I drop in to the estate agent's, handing over the spare set of keys, then head over Kew Bridge to turn west and join the M4. Approaching Heathrow, I spot queuing traffic. A year ago that would have been me, stuck in the back of a cab, working away, not bothering to so much as glance up until I reached the terminal. It feels great to be leaving it all behind.

Once on the M25, I see the signs for Iver Heath, the turnoff for Pinewood Studios. I'd gone to Pinewood to meet the production team working on *The Making of 101 Dalmatians* while the movie of *101 Dalmatians*, starring

Glenn Close was being filmed. I couldn't wait to finish the meeting as I was as awestruck as any kid, gawping at the lavish set in all its spooky cobwebby glory. It was my first time on the set of a big-budget Hollywood film and I couldn't get over the sheer scale of it. But it was the chance to meet the four-legged stars rather than the two-legged ones that I couldn't resist. I glance at Zebedee, curled up in her favourite position in the passenger footwell.

I'll take one Labrador over 101 Dalmatians any day, cute as they were.

A week later, the estate agent rings me to say that two young professionals, one of whom is a researcher on *This Morning,* are interested in renting the flat. She sends me their references and I agree immediately; they're just what I'm looking for.

They sign the lease for a year. I pay the agency to find the tenants and deal with the lease, but the day-to-day management is down to me. Worried that I'm having to manage the flat remotely as it's a four-hour drive away should something go wrong, I've assembled a team of tradespeople who will fix things at short notice. I expect to pay over the odds for their services, but it saves me both the hassle and the cost in petrol of having to deal with problems in person.

Now that I have guaranteed regular money coming in, I relax. But it's short lived. Three months later, my neighbour from the upstairs flat phones me.

'Look, there's something you should know about those girls downstairs...'

Don't tell me: they're too good to be true.

'What's happened?'

'There are some dodgy-looking guys who come to the

door late at night. I hear them shouting at the girls. Sounds threatening. They don't stay long before leaving again.'

On paper, my tenants are young women who grew up in the Home Counties and work in well-paid jobs. But low-lifes dropping around in the middle of the night? I was surrounded by the drugs and sex trade when I lived next to Sydney's red light district. All the girls and boys who sold sex there did so to finance their drug habit.

A few days later, I receive a call from my bank warning me that I am in danger of being unable to honour my mortgage payment. I'm numb with shock.

'But there's a direct debit that comes in every month for £725 from my tenants. I checked it yesterday and it was in the account.'

'You're right, it came in, but the sending bank reversed the transaction,' the banker says.

'But how come?'

'There aren't sufficient funds in the sender's account to honour the payment,' the woman says gently.

'What do I do?' I'm thinking aloud now.

'I'd contact your tenants immediately, if I were you.'

'I'll transfer the payment from another account. Thanks for letting me know.'

This can't be happening.

I compose myself before I pick up the phone to the tenants. There's no point in being angry. That won't pay my mortgage. I get voicemail and leave a message.

'I'll give you seven days to come up with the rent you owe me, so let me know how you intend to pay me back.'

Minutes later, I get a call from a number I don't recognise.

'How dare you hassle my daughter for money like that,' shouts an imperious-sounding woman.

Who do you think you are? The Duchess of Chiswick?

'I'm sorry, I don't think we've been introduced.'

'I'm Candice's mother,' the woman says, curtly. Ah, Candice. One of my troublesome tenants.

'I can't pay my mortgage because your daughter hasn't paid her rent. What do you suggest I do?'

'That's your problem,' the woman snaps.

Victim blaming now, are we? Making out I'm the problem? Woman, you have no shame.

'You've got their deposit. Use that,' the wannabe Duchess says.

'And what happens after that's run out?' I'm met with silence. 'I'll use their deposit, providing they're out by the end of the week—leaving the property as they found it,' I continue. 'I'll meet them there on Friday at 1pm when they can hand over the keys.'

'Suit yourself,' the Duchess snaps.

'I know what's going on here,' I say, brazening it out. After all, the Duchess has set this tone for the conversation. 'Candice and her friend's late-night visitors—male visitors — are disturbing my neighbours. And I'm not stupid.'

'Candice will be admitted to the Priory on Saturday,' the Duchess says, making it sound like her daughter has just won a place at Oxbridge.

So it was drugs after all. And if you can afford to send your daughter to the Priory for rehab, why won't you pay her debts?

The Priory is a luxury clinic where the moneyed and the stars go to detox. There's a rumour that it's a great place to pitch a script to a captive audience, although you would have to be very devious to sneak in there.

On Friday, I drive down from Liverpool and wait for Candice and co to turn up. A Mercedes pulls up in the tiny street and the driver leaves it there, double-parked. Out spill my soon-to-be-ex-tenants, accompanied by the wannabe Duchess sporting a Piaget watch and expensive diamonds. She looks at me down her imperious nose as though I'm the scullery maid.

'Here,' the Duchess says, practically throwing the keys at me.

The two girls look sheepish, glancing at me every now and again. The one not related to the Duchess mumbles, 'Sorry.'

What am I supposed to say? Have a good detox?

As they drive off, I go inside, checking for any damage. To be fair to them, they have left the place spotless. I've been lucky. Their dealers could so easily have trashed the flat when the girls could no longer afford to pay for their drugs. But I don't have enough savings to keep up the payments when times are bad. It could take me weeks to find new tenants, and I'd still have the constant worry of having to fork out for repairs.

When I arrive home, I'm surprised to get a call from one of my upstairs neighbour's friends who says she's interested in "taking the flat off my hands."

I listen to her spiel. 'I've always wanted to buy in Kew.'

Fair enough.

'I do have an offer for you. I'm a cash buyer so you wouldn't have to pay commission to an estate agent, and the sale could be done and dusted in a couple of weeks.'

The offer is too low and I decline it. She's very pushy. I tell her I'll think about it.

I ring around various estate agents, inviting three to give me an estimate of the property's value. Then I call Miss Pushy back and say I'll speak to her again after the estate agents have been round. My intention is to take the middle estimate as my starting point for negotiations. She seems surprised by this; I imagine she's used to getting her own way, with enough inherited wealth at the grand age of 25 to make a cash offer on a flat in Kew.

I've run television budgets ten times the amount you're offering. I'm not quite the pushover you thought.

A few days later, I receive the estimates and call her.

'If you raise your offer, minus the selling fees, you've got yourself a deal.'

'But I'm giving you cash,' she says.

'You are. But I'm selling this at a very fair price. It's up to you. I have three agents falling over themselves to sell it on my behalf.'

I am bluffing. I don't want to put the property on the open market in case it takes too long to sell. And I'd have to take a loan out to cover the mortgage in the interim. She duly raises her offer.

Phew!

I'm not giving up on an investment property, I just need something closer to home. I've made a decent profit in two years, but want a newly converted flat in a block which requires less maintenance than Kew. And my opportunity comes sooner than I expected when I'm offered a job-share in Artists' Contracts at BBC Manchester which, although part- time, is a permanent role.

My application for a buy-to-let loan on a two-bed warehouse conversion in a former cotton mill is successful. Property up here is much cheaper than in London and I use the profit from the Kew sale to reduce my mortgage. What's more, the office is five minutes' walk away on Oxford Road and any problems can be sorted out in my lunch hour or after work.

I am attracted to my new post for the hours and the opportunity to work in what I assumed was an exclusive club, not open to the likes of me. I imagined the entry level requirement would be a law degree, specialising in media law, but I get the job offer because of my experience of contracting television talent and supervising productions. If only Mum was still around. She could at last stand up and say with confidence to her friends, 'Alison works for the BBC.'

It's not my dream job, Mum, but now I'm in, I'm hoping I can move into something more creative than being at the sharp end of Talent Management, negotiating contracts with agents. Are you writing all this down?

My job sharer has been at the corporation for years. She chooses to work Monday to Wednesday lunchtime. We have an hour's handover, and then I take over for the latter half of the week. She leaves me copious Post-it notes on the various contracts and the stage of the negotiations. I spend the first couple of hours familiarising myself with any fresh developments, ready to pick up the phone and resume the process.

It doesn't take me long to realise that requests for talent from production departments come in at the last minute on a Friday afternoon. The most nerve-wracking part of a job share for me is tidying up and ensuring that all the notes I leave for my colleague are clear. She is meticulous and neat, and I'm the opposite. But even when it's buried under a mountain of paperwork, I know where everything is.

I often stay later than 5.30pm as all I'd be doing otherwise is sitting in rush-hour traffic. One evening, my boss pulls me aside.

'They don't pay us enough to do voluntary overtime.'
'Even if Entertainment puts in an urgent request at 5.30pm on a Friday?'

'Especially then. Tell them it has to wait until Monday.'

The last thing I want to be known as is a jobsworth, but if

this is the attitude of management, I suppose I'd better agree to go along with it. For now. It's no wonder my junior colleagues are such a crack team of clock-watchers who start putting away files at five, then spend the next half an hour tidying their desks.

After a year, the BBC offers me a permanent full-time position when a colleague relocates to Birmingham. Not long after that, my boss retires and HR offers me the job of Head of Contracts at BBC North. I accept the promotion and the pay rise that goes with it, not realising that the man I am replacing started on a far higher salary than me.

As the boss, I'm now the line-manager of the jobsworths, who tag-team their sick days so that they can take a Friday off when it suits them. Which is practically every other week. When I arrive at work, there will be a message left on voicemail, saying one of the terrible trio is feeling poorly and won't be coming in that day. The one who's been there the longest—for over twenty years—has found all the loopholes. For a single day's absence, an employee can "self-certify" their sickness. It's only after three days continuous absence that they need to provide a doctor's certificate. It must be a great feeling to skive off on the busiest day of the week, knowing your colleagues will be left in the lurch.

To mix it up a bit, they'll take the occasional Monday off.

But not once, in all the time I've been there, have any of them been off sick on any other days. I contact HR, asking if I can check absenteeism records for the previous five years, as I'm worried about all their absences. The Deputy Head of HR, her face as pale as an undercooked Greggs' pasty, stares at me through her fringe like I just walked into her office and told her Blur are better than Oasis.

'I wouldn't rock the boat if I were you,' she tells me curtly.

I walk out of HR in a state of shock.

Did I hear that right? Sounds like a threat. What have I got myself into here?

I sit looking out on to the street below, mulling over the fact management won't support me. It looks like I'll just have to tackle the problem myself. A social acquaintance who happens to be an occupational psychologist advises me to address the issue through the weekly Monday team meeting. Whichever slacker is due to take this Friday off will no doubt hope their absence will be forgotten by Monday. The way to tackle it, my psychologist friend suggests, is to have a strategy of accountability at the meeting, asking her two colleagues what the impact of her absenteeism has been on their workload.

I have a quiet word with the other Contract Executives in the office, advising them of my intentions. They back me all the way, relieved that someone is finally tackling the sick leave issue.

I'm nervous at the next Monday meeting, but try my best not to show it. Friday's absentee tries to brazen it out; she can probably see what I'm up to as she's the smartest one of the trio, but the other two, who aren't quite as bright, admit that they struggled to keep up with the workload that day. This proves to be effective. Once the terrible trio gets the idea into their heads that their actions have consequences, the absenteeism becomes far less of a problem than it was when I first started.

One-nil to me.

Now that I'm full-time, I no longer have the freedom or the emotional energy to write. The whole reason for applying for a job-share was to have the headspace for writing.

You've only got yourself to blame, I tell myself. *You let your ambition get in the way.*

By the time I get home after work, I'm wrung out. My routine goes like this: leave the house at 8am with Zebedee, drop her off with the dog-minder, then I follow the scenic route, passing through the hidden villages of the Wirral until I reach the M53. Thirty minutes in, approximately twenty miles from home, I get to Ellesmere Port. To my left is the post-apocalyptic mass of grey pipework that is the Stanlow Oil Refinery. It takes ten minutes to drive past the vast complex, roughly the size of 300 football pitches.

As I drive towards Manchester airport, the long line of vehicles slows down and speeds up until there's the inevitable crash as one car goes into the back of another. Near the airport, the traffic is backed up all the way to Oxford Road. I often hear the roar of a sports car behind me, checking my rear-view mirror as the driver pushes past. Another Maserati. South Manchester is Premier League footballer territory, but the only face I'd recognise is David Beckham's. No matter how powerful that car is, they're still not getting through the traffic any faster than me.

An hour and a half after leaving home, I arrive at the office. And between 5.30 and 6pm, I drive home. At night, the dirty snaking steel pipes at Stanlow magically disappear to be replaced by a spectacular light show that would give Walt Disney World's Christmas display a run for its money. As the twinkling lights fade into the distance, I'm nearly home. I go to collect my darling Zebedee who, despite her hectic day at doggy daycare, greets me as though it was months, not hours since I last saw her. After a busy week, my weekends are for dog walking and socialising.

One plus about working for the BBC is that the corporation takes management training seriously. I'm sent off on various courses covering negotiation skills and dealing with difficult people—we certainly have plenty of those in the office. As for the contract negotiations, they can go on for weeks. No matter how much money the agent asks for or what conditions they try to impose, the basic negotiation is always the same: the artist's agent demands roughly twice as much as our first offer. If the agent thinks that the job is right for their client, they meet us halfway.

We can't compete with the eye-watering fees paid by advertiser-funded broadcasters as we can't be seen to waste licence-payers' money. While we don't negotiate too far on fees, we can throw in various sweeteners depending on the star power of the talent. There's room for negotiation on the wardrobe budget or whether they can bring in their own make-up artist. But what it boils down to is whether the agent (or the artist) wants the job or not. And even after all the moaning and complaining, they rarely say no.

The negotiations I dread the most are with one particular agent who eats contract executives for breakfast. I wonder why she spends so much energy on shooting down the messengers, which is all we are. She knows exactly how far to push me, switching on the charm at the last minute, just before the deal is about to fall over. She must love the chase, but it leaves me cold.

It isn't just clients with agents who make life difficult. Many successful radio broadcasters represent themselves and waste time haggling over £50 like second-rate used-car dealers. The rudest man I ever had to contract is a historian and academic who seemed to relish bullying and belittling me. But like most bullies, he went too far eventually and got his comeuppance when two universities and a publisher severed all ties with him over his outrageous racist remarks.

It may be tough negotiating with talent in the UK, but

it's a whole other ball game dealing with celebrities in the USA. Across the pond, there are more layers of gatekeepers than I thought possible. To get to the talent I want, I may have to consult an entertainment lawyer, a manager and an agent, who all have to agree.

At Christmas, the BBC makes a clip show, showing archive footage from the biggest TV hits of the 1980s. One is a clip from *Dallas*, a series I loved starring Larry Hagman as Oil Baron JR Ewing and Linda Gray as his long-suffering wife Sue Ellen. It is 5 in the afternoon UK time and I'm dreading calling Los Angeles, where it's 9am. I dial the number, expecting to be fobbed off by any one of half a dozen gate- keepers.

'Larry Hagman,' drawls a familiar Texan voice. I nearly fall off my chair. JR Ewing himself is at home in Southfork, answering his own phone? I run through my spiel and he listens politely. 'Sure, that sounds great,' he says. This is going so well; beyond my wildest dreams, in fact. Convinced my offer will fall apart when I tell him about the money, I plough on.

'The fee for the extract is the standard BBC rate for two broadcasts.'

Surely the boss of Ewing Oil will say, 'Hell, no.'

'I'm honoured that the BBC still remembers our little show,' he says with a chuckle. I leave work on a high that day and think about the different ways in which the great and the good treat the "little" people. It reveals their real character, and unlike the selfish JR, Larry Hagman has proved himself to be a true gentleman.

Truth sometimes being more far-fetched than fiction preoccupies me the next day when I arrive at work to be met by a voice message from one of the terrible trio.

'I won't be in today. Irene will tell you what happened.' And with that, she hangs up.

That's original. It's Thursday. Or is she taking a very long weekend?

As I walk out of my office, along the corridor and towards the secretaries' desks, I glance through the glass partition and see Irene hanging up her coat. I don't want to ambush her as she's only just arrived, but she walks straight up to me.

'Jodie's sick.'

'She just left a message,' I say, trying to keep the sarcasm out of my voice.

This had better be good.

'Her whole family's in Manchester Royal Infirmary. And she put them in there.'

What did she do? Lay them out with a few left hooks?

'What happened?'

'Her mam asked her to go out to the garden and pick some flowers to make the salad look pretty. Because it was dark, she picked foxgloves instead of nasturtiums and they ate the lot. There were ambulances and everything, and now they're all on drips.'

This is so far-fetched, it must be true.

'Oh dear,' is all I manage. 'I hope they'll be alright.'

And luckily, they are and the absences dwindle yet again.

Until, that is, Jodie announces she's pregnant.

Here we go. She's going to milk this one for all it's worth.

But it will no longer be my problem. In November 2000, Seán and I plus one Labrador fly from cold, rainy Manchester airport to a new life Down Under.

23

Back to the Future

New Zealand
Before I left film school, I sat down with director Maciej and discussed the possibility of working together again. We have kept in touch and he updates me with how he is trying to raise the finance to make my screenplay of *Day Return/Waves*, a love story set on the last day of an affair, into a short film. In the story, a woman tells her lover that she is leaving town forever to join her husband abroad.

In 2005, Maciej gets in touch again, telling me that not only has he raised the funds, but the film has been acquired by Polish Television.

Most short films are made on a shoestring with very low production values. All the money raised has to be spent on getting the film made, leaving the crew and writer with nothing apart from out-of-pocket expenses. This is a properly funded production which allows for a composer to create the music and work with professional musicians; one of Europe's leading cinematographers to shoot it; and established actors to play the main characters. And not only that,

I am to be paid for the screenplay and the broadcasting rights. I am beyond delighted and can scarcely contain my excitement. To think that after all these years, this project will finally see the light of day!

The production company sends me the contract and I have it vetted by the UK Writers' Guild. I look over some old BBC notes, comparing my offer with their rates. It's very favourable. I accept the deal.

When I see the completed film for the first time, I'm swept along by the drama. I can't quite believe how the setting, a small seaside town on the South Coast of England in the 1960s, has been re-imagined so inventively as 1980s Gdansk, Poland. Given the brilliant job that Maciej has made of my script, I offer to help submit the film to foreign film festivals.

Since I left Disney, I've had an idea percolating. It's an image of the oil refinery at Stanlow—how the place, so dirty and uninspiring by daylight, is transformed into a magical wonderland at night. It would make a brilliant film location. And it turns out that Seán's been having the same thoughts too. He wants us to co-write an eco-thriller screenplay, and what better place to set it than an oil refinery? We've never thought about co-writing before, but as we have different areas of expertise and complementary skills, we are able to come up with an outline which we work on together for the next two years.

The momentum for *Day Return/Waves* builds and it is included as part of the official selection at a number of film festivals across Europe, including the prestigious St Petersburg Film Festival in Russia. In 2007 it wins the Special Jury Award at WorldFest in Houston. There are invitations to other festivals, including some in the United States that

Maciej and I would love to attend, but neither of us can afford to go. As there's nothing left in the budget for international marketing, we would have to pay for the airfares and accommodation out of our own pockets.

We do, however, plan to travel to at least one competitive international festival where there are paid awards up for grabs and we can meet with potential funders for future projects. We receive an enthusiastic yes from the Hollywood Very Short Movies Festival, even though a 25-minute film is a "long" short. Maciej plans to go as the festival is not only going to screen the film, but will run an intensive programme for both producers and directors to meet leading Hollywood agents, managers and script executives. He's such a talented director, he deserves to hit the big time.

Two weeks before Maciej is due to leave, I receive an email from him to say that because of an illness in the family, he can't travel. Will I go in his place? I grab the opportunity with both hands. The organisers are relieved that one of us is going to be there to take audience questions after the screenings and seem amenable to my attending the workshops in Maciej's place.

Then they check that I have a film project to pitch. Do I *what*? Seán and I have been working together on the screenplay outline for *Revolution Earth*, our fast-paced eco-thriller set in Australia, Antarctica and Europe. It's shaping up nicely, so yes, I do have a film to pitch.

I fly from Auckland to LA the day before the event starts and stay at the Holiday Inn Express & Suites on North Highlands Avenue. It's the cheapest hotel I can find within walking distance of Grauman's Egyptian Theatre, the legendary Hollywood movie palace where the festival is being held. Even so, it costs me $1,250 for five nights; at least the tariff includes breakfast, so the only meal I need to worry about is dinner as subsidised lunches are on offer at the venue.

My room is on the fifth floor, facing North Highlands Avenue, a busy road. It comes with air-conditioning, which I use not to keep the room cool, but to drown out the hum of the all-night traffic. On my first evening in LA, I struggle to find anywhere close by that serves anything other than fast food. I'm just around the corner from the Hollywood & Highland shopping mall and hope there'll be somewhere that can sell me something healthy—this is the town that practically invented the egg-white omelette after all—but there's nothing to be had. Luckily, the Spanish-speaking staff of the hotel restaurant are incredibly helpful, once they get over their surprise that a guest would bother to ask their advice.

'We can make you something,' the waiter says. 'I'll ask the chef. Do you like spice?'

'Do I like spice? I was born in South East Asia.' The chef brings me a delicious Mexican chicken dish with freshly made tortillas and sides of beans and guacamole.

The next day after breakfast, excited but nervous, I set off for the festival. It's only 500 metres, but there's a no-man's- land area I have to pass, which is sadly full of homeless people, camped out in tents on the sidewalk. I've watched movies about what happens when the American dream goes sour, but the reality is confronting. And after a lengthy day, I confess I cross over to the other side of the street once it gets dark.

After midnight, the temperature has dropped fifteen degrees. Following a warm day of 25C, it feels like it's below zero. I haven't eaten dinner and the only place open is a fast-food restaurant giving out free food and coffee to the homeless. I always thought that fast-food joints were just anonymous corporate entities, but at this outlet, at least, somebody has compassion.

The third day sees the *Day Return/Waves* screening. I worry that a subtitled film will put the paying audience off, so I'm delighted when I look around to discover the theatre filling up. This is only the second time in my life that I've sat with an audience at a screening of a film I've written, choosing the back row to watch their reaction. I'm seeing the film on a big screen for the first time, just as they are, and I feel like I'm watching it through their eyes. I recognise my story and the translated dialogue, but the seaside setting of Gdansk is other worldly. It's somewhere I will never be likely to visit.

At the Q&A, there's such warmth and enthusiasm towards the film that I walk out of that auditorium feeling proud. What Maciej has achieved is so amazing, it's sad that he isn't here to witness it.

The day after the screening, I tag along with nine of the directors as we head off to the pitching workshop being held at the Hollywood Roosevelt Hotel, no less. The hotel is on Hollywood Boulevard and since 1927 has played host to all manner of screen legends, including Errol Flynn and Marilyn Monroe. We're invited to lunch to meet the power brokers. At a long table, we're served the most delicious three-course meal, which I barely touch as I'm so nervous. All I think about is my pitch.

With lunch over, we get on to business. We're ushered out to the pool area and briefed on the format. It will be run like speed-dating where we'll pitch our projects to one executive at a time, then move on to the next. To quell my nerves, I check out the Tropicana pool, which has a mural painted by none other than David Hockney. It's extraordinary to see the real thing, there below the shimmering water. I want to dive in, but remember why I'm here and return to my seat, a pool-side lounge chair, while I wait for the great and the good to take their places.

Most of the executives, especially the women, wear dark sunglasses. My opening line, 'It's an eco-thriller set on four continents, including Antarctica', seems to go okay. Or they're being polite. But then I spoil it by adding too much detail.

Do it the way they do in The Player.

One of my favourite movies, *The Player* is an insider's view about the way writers are treated in Hollywood. I recall the scene where the writer pitches a screenplay to a producer in a lift because he's told he has to do it in 60 seconds or fewer. It's also a thriller about a producer who murders a screenwriter and gets away with it. I let that be a lesson for me.

After the fourth or fifth pitch, I'm getting into the swing of things, enjoying myself. Then I wait expectantly for the feedback from the executive in front of me.

There's an awkward silence.

'Australia, you say? Like *Crocodile Dundee*?'

Crocodile Dundee? Is that her only cultural reference? I'm screwed if so.

'Australia, yes, that's the whole third act. It's not tropical North Queensland, but down south. Where there aren't any crocodiles,' I end lamely. I can't see her eyes through her designer sunglasses, but I bet they're glazed over. And it's the same with the following three pitches: I may as well be speaking to the mural at the bottom of the pool. Nobody in LA cares about what goes on in other countries. The story will have to be moved to North

America—this is the message coming through loud and clear.

My last pitch is to an executive from Fox Searchlight. He listens to what I have to say. Maybe because he's African-American, the indigenous cultural themes in both the New Zealand and Australian settings seem to interest him. He takes off his sunglasses and looks me in the eye.

'Write it as a novel first,' he says. 'That way, you hold on to the creative vision. And if someone wants to make a movie out of it, they'll have to pay you for the rights.'

That's the most important piece of advice I take away with me from my time in Hollywood. I leave LA, vowing that I've had enough of writing screenplays that will never see the light of day.

* * *

I begin a new day job as a Corporate Relocation Consultant, working with new arrivals to Auckland, helping them find a place to live. It's similar to location scouting for films, only there's an added layer of psychology involved. Often what the client says they want and what they really want aren't the same, so I try to establish what's driving the relocation.

With couples, I observe their body language to see whether they're both on board with the move. If not, I try to find out why. The job is part-time and gives me the space not only to write, but to return to university and pick up where I left off in the Art History course I abandoned as an undergraduate. It's a matter of pride. I don't like starting something and not finishing, even though there were perfectly understandable reasons behind it. I was in denial about Dad's death and pushed on, but when it was clear I couldn't continue, going home was the right decision.

I repeat the first year of Italian Classical and Renaissance Art and Architecture at the University of Auckland. When the slides come up in class, I recognise many of the paintings and sculptures that I was lucky enough to see in real life when I lived in Florence. I love art history so much, I take a second-year paper, Northern Renaissance Art. I'm not doing it for a particular purpose. Not at the time, anyway.

As well as studying, I write a non-fiction book proposal and send it to a Publisher in Oxford who specialises in books about travel and moving abroad. I'm offered a two-book deal for *Buying a House in New Zealand* and *Retiring to Australia and New Zealand*, paid advances and given nine months to complete them both. Then my Publisher retires and his backlist is acquired by a company specialising in business books that no longer wishes to publish the list I write for. I find this out when my name and biography disappear from the website; the company didn't even do me the courtesy of informing me. And I thought it was just television that was cut-throat.

I get useful advice from the Alliance of Independent Authors about seeking the return of my intellectual property rights for my books from my Publisher. After gaining the rights back, I am now free to self-publish, which makes me realise I can do this without a third party taking a cut of my earnings.

Seán and I complete the novel of the environmental thriller *Revolution Earth* and write the second book in the series, *Nighthawks*, about looted art and antiquities in Italy. Far from wasting four months in Florence on holiday, I absorb the culture and carry out research for this novel, which is finally published in 2021. I am Co-writer, Producer,

Set- designer and Director, and what's more, I own the intellectual property in my work.

I think back to all those years of singing to someone else's tune, the humiliations in the workplace and being beholden to my corporate masters. There I was, so busy trying to prove to myself that I could be someone when the answer was there all the time. And that it's me, finally getting to call all the shots.

Author Note

Thanks so much for reading this book. If you enjoyed it, I would love it if you would leave a review on your favourite book review website. It doesn't have to be a long one. Even a line or two makes all the difference.

Acknowledgments

For Jody Lawless without whom I would never have moved to Sydney; for Teri Sawers for her wise counsel about going to London. To Marianne Sheehan for introducing me to the best temping agency. And above all to Fran Triefus and Anita Bennett. If it wasn't for you two, I'd still be working at that trade information service in Bond Street. Thank you to Dymphna Callery who braved snarling dogs to join me on our writing journey.

I am so grateful to Alison Jack for her meticulous and generous developmental and copy editing. Once again, I am very fortunate to have the input of beta reader Stephanie Light, who read the manuscript not once but twice and saved me from making many embarrassing mistakes.

Thanks once again to Andrew Brown of Design for Writers for his imaginative book cover, which perfectly captures the tone of this memoir.

And most of all, my heartfelt thanks go to Seán for all his hard graft at the day job, without which I'd never be able to write full-time.

About the Author

Alison Ripley Cubitt is a multi-genre author. She is part of the crime fighting duo, Lambert Nagle. She co-writes international thrillers, mystery and crime under this pseudonym with Seán Cubitt, who also happens to be her trophy husband.

For the past two years, she has divided her time between home and the shops—all within the permitted five-kilometre radius. But in 2022, she hopes to travel further afield and finally get to use at least one of her three passports.

In her downtime, Alison volunteers with St Kilda Doggy Daycare and is a fully paid-up member of the Organisation for Australasian Insomniacs.

Misadventures in the Screen Trade is Alison's eighth book. Keep in touch with Alison on the web: https://www.lambertnagle.com

Also by Alison Ripley Cubitt

Castles in the Air: A Family Memoir of Love and Loss

Buying a House in New Zealand: Find Your Perfect Home

Blue Silk Dress in *Mosaics 2:* (A Collection of Independent Women)

If you love reading and writing memoirs, join us in the We Love Memoirs Facebook group.

www.facebook.com/groups/welovememoirs

www.ingramcontent.com/pod-product-compliance
Lightning Source LLC
Chambersburg PA
CBHW051558010526
44118CB00023B/2740